Everyday Mantras

First published in 2022 by Rock Point, an imprint of The Quarto Group,
142 West 36th Street, 4th Floor, New York, NY 10018, USA
T (212) 779-4972 | F (212) 779-6058 | www.Quarto.com

Rock Point titles are also available at discount for retail, wholesale, promotional, and bulk purchase. For
details, contact the Special Sales Manager by email at specialsales@quarto.com or by mail at The Quarto
Group, Attn: Special Sales Manager, 100 Cummings Center Suite 265D, Beverly, MA 01915, USA.

Library of Congress Cataloging-in-Publication Data

Names: Gunar, Aysel, author.
Title: Everyday mantras : 365 affirmations for happiness, strength, and peace / Aysel Gunar.
Description: New York : Rock Point, 2022. | Summary: "Everyday Mantras
  gives you 365 seasonal mantras and meditations for a year filled with
  awakened awareness"-- Provided by publisher.
Identifiers: LCCN 2021007964 (print) | LCCN 2021007965 (ebook) | ISBN
  9781631067662 (hardcover) | ISBN 9781631067679 (ebook)
Subjects: LCSH: Self-consciousness (Awareness) | Mantras. |
  Self-acceptance.
Classification: LCC BF311 .G793 2021 (print) | LCC BF311 (ebook) | DDC
  153--dc23
LC record available at https://lccn.loc.gov/2021007964
LC ebook record available at https://lccn.loc.gov/2021007965

10 9 8 7 6 5 4

ISBN: 978-1-63106-766-2

Publisher: Rage Kindelsperger
Creative Director: Laura Drew
Managing Editor: Cara Donaldson
Project Editor: Leeann Moreau
Interior Design: Amy Harte for 3&Co.

Printed in China

Everyday Mantras

365 Affirmations for Happiness, Strength, and Peace

Aysel Gunar

Founder of

mantraband®

ROCK
POINT

Contents

Use this book
to create a ritual

This book is designed for you to read daily, checking in
with the corresponding date each morning or evening as
a moment of reflection. If you'd like to bring the spirit of
the daily contemplation through to your whole day, you
can read this book in the morning in a quiet moment with
a cup of tea or coffee. If you prefer, you can reach for
the daily dose of reflection at the end of your day instead,
ideally once you've wound down and decompressed from
the busyness of life.

You may find that it is helpful to integrate a journaling
practice into your reading and reflecting. It may even
be useful to incorporate additional time meditating
on the phrases, their extended descriptions, and your
own thoughts after reading. Let it create a moment of
stillness, gentleness, and generosity for your spirit. Take
it with you into your daily life to widen the horizons of
your heart each day.

January

JANUARY 1
Claim a fresh start

A new year that starts on the first of January is as arbitrary as one that starts on the twenty-second of June, but that doesn't make the ritual of the calendar new year any less powerful. The new year we all honor together has the weight of intention that every one of us invests in it. Treat this clean slate as a choice to be made, rather than a forced march toward change. You can be the same person in the new year if you want. You can change one thing. You can change more if you desire, but there is no obligation. Start whenever and wherever you are.

JANUARY 2
Make a resolution

What have you resolved to do? Whether you made a list yesterday or three months ago, or never made a list at all, you have things you want to do and be. Resolutions are just intentions, choices you make to honor your desire to change and be better. They don't require perfection, or even demand all of your commitment. But a resolution asks you to take a chance and try to chase after something you want. It is not a promise, nor is there any particular consequence if you don't achieve the goal. It's simply an invitation. Will you take it?

JANUARY 3
Give yourself permission to pause

Have you given yourself permission to pause? It's not easy to give yourself a moment to rest. But it's okay to slow down. Your life can contain so much busyness, so much urgency and movement. The difficulty lies in choosing when to pause and then appreciating all of that movement in its absence. When the world pauses, allow yourself to pause with it. Everyone deserves these moments, and you deserve these moments, too.

JANUARY 4
Have courage

What are you waiting for? It's all well and good to chase things when they thrill you, but to chase the things that scare you is something else. There is no shame in fear, but you should not let it stop you from taking action. Your courage comes from running through the flames into new adventures. You do not need to set aside your fear. Let it be your companion if you need it. But leap anyway, even if you are holding hands with your fears to do so. Fly with bravery!

JANUARY 5
Use your tools

Your hands are not empty; they are full of tools and resources at your disposal. If you feel alone or ill equipped, sit back and consider what you might be missing. Who can help you take the next step, guide you forward, or give you advice? What latent talent or forgotten skill might help you solve your problem? You have the resources you need to move forward.

JANUARY 6
Be patient with the winter

The days are short and cold, but that does not mean they cannot be filled with joy. Winter is an opportunity to slow down, connect with our homes and ourselves, reflect on what we will do when the sun emerges again. Find ways to use your hands and occupy the long evenings. Enjoy the cozy feeling of socks, of blankets and sweaters and hot beverages. There are plenty of joys to be found in the cold, both indoors and out. Embrace the cycle of the seasons, and lean into the specific joys of winter.

JANUARY 7
Make plans

When life slows down, it is time to catch your breath and recharge. Your body needs the slow procession of the seasons, a time for energetic activity and a time to plan for the future. You do not need to be busy at every moment, creating and growing and stretching against limits. Even ambition needs time to percolate and coalesce into solid dreams and plans. Give yourself over to making plans, rather than carrying them out.

JANUARY 8
Don't let perfection stop you

Perfect is the enemy of completion. It's noble to want to achieve your goals perfectly, to want to be perfectly good or perfectly capable, but it's not possible. Don't let a desire to pursue total perfection stop you from moving forward. Our imperfections are what make us human, and what build bridges between us. They are useful in their own way. You cannot shed them entirely, so look for ways to embrace them as an asset.

JANUARY 9
Allow yourself to be loose

Open your jaws wide, dropping your tongue away from
the roof of your mouth. Roll your shoulders in their
sockets, shaking free your shoulder blades. Gently tilt
your head side to side, stretching your neck. Can you
feel the release? So much of the tension and emotional
load we carry is stored in our bodies, even when we are
processing it in our heart. The body knows what you feel;
it holds it for you to support you. Make sure you stretch
out your limbs. Wiggle your joints, extend your body in
space, and shake the tension free.

JANUARY 10
Build your patience

How long it can take for things expected to arrive at
their designated hour! The moments of waiting need not
be an empty vacuum—even anticipation and desire can be
full of exquisite value and joy. Slowly the things we need
and want come to us, but the waiting can be difficult.
Cultivating patience can be a reward in and of itself.
Anticipation has its own sweetness. The present moment
moves quickly and slowly in turns.

JANUARY 11
Let there be quiet

Drifting through the sky, gentle and light. Did you know that snow has a vital function in our winter landscape? It's not just decorative; snow insulates the plants and animals that sleep beneath it. Many creatures and foliage need a specific time in hibernation or cold-induced stasis in order to flourish in the spring. You too need a period of quiet to thrive.

JANUARY 12
Keep warm

What do you do to keep your body warm? You likely have favorite socks, a beloved coat or sweater, a favorite hot beverage to sip on during cold nights. A hot bath or shower warms frozen limbs and loosens knotted muscles. What do you do to warm your heart on days when it feels chilled to the core? Do you have coping mechanisms you return to like a favorite pair of sweatpants? Look for the things that warm your soul like soup warms your belly—a good book, the voice of a friend, a movie seen a thousand times. Keep them handy the way you would a perfect pair of gloves. Your heart needs care in the winter as much as your body does.

JANUARY 13
Color is everywhere

Winter is known for its white icing, bare branches, and gray skies, but this season can shine with color as much as any other. The green of pines and red of berries, the blazing blue of a bright and sunny sky, even the yellow glow of the full moon in the night can color your season. Look for the flash of the wings of the birds who stay through the season or the golden rays of an afternoon. Let them be the blooms that sustain you in the chill.

JANUARY 14
Embrace your strength

You have pushed through difficulty, muscled your way through moments. Your goals wait for you along the road you are walking, not at the end; they are milestones you can and will reach. Resilience and strength are important to the journey, but so is commitment and willpower. What you need is inside you, pushing you forward. Keep reaching.

JANUARY 15
Ask for less

We are constantly told to ask for more, to expand our desires to fill the world and claim the limits of our wants. What would happen if you asked for less? You will never satisfy an ever-expanding desire; chasing fulfillment with no limit is constantly inviting the world to disappoint you. Instead, invite in gratitude for what you have in your life and the wonderful things that are already within reach. You do not have to make your heart small to do this; you only have to widen the scope of what it means to be fulfilled.

JANUARY 16
Look for guidance

Each of us feels lost and confused at some point in our lives. When it happens to you, rest assured that you are in the best company possible. When you need encouragement, turn back the pages of history and let the people who have come before you lead you forward. There are many ways of finding your way through and putting your feet on a new path. Look for people in the past who have gotten late starts on their journeys, who have wandered through complicated circumstances or enormous challenges. You are not alone.

JANUARY 17
The stars still shine

Are there stars above you now? If you cannot see them, try to envision them in your mind. They are always above you, whirling in ancient arcs that have seen the rise and fall of entire civilizations. Imprints of fading, brilliant light are brightest when it is darkest with all other lights turned low. While the dark can inspire fear, it can also reveal the most beautiful and intricate galaxies of the universe. The path of the stars is long, and constant. Let them guide you.

JANUARY 18
Ambition is a path

Your dreams are a healthy part of what makes you who you are. Wanting to become more, to achieve more, is a constructive impulse that helps make the world a better place and creates our collective future. It is through our dreams that we build and stretch the limits of the possible. Pay attention to where these goals fuel and inspire you, and when they might leave you feeling burned out and empty. You do not need to chase a goal that is no longer meaningful or fulfilling. Follow-through is important, but not at the expense of your heart.

JANUARY 19
Act

What may happen may still happen yet—no one knows what the future holds, or when our hopes and dreams will bear fruit. If you want to increase the likelihood of your preferred future, it will require your action to shift the balance. You cannot be certain of the outcome, but you can tip the scales in your favor through the choices you make. Do not rely on hope alone to make the future; you are capable of so much more than that.

JANUARY 20
Keep hoping

The world changes, ebbs and flows. What is happening
in this moment will pass, replaced by a new moment.
Reach out your hands to the next moment. It needs you
and your hope in what comes next. Hope can be fragile,
joyful, or anxious. It does not always feel like relief, but
it's necessary all the same. Keep it safe in your heart, and
move forward with it.

JANUARY 21
Every action has consequences

Some consequences are easily predicted; others are entirely unpredictable as we watch our actions spin us into the universe. We are free to make choices, but not free from the consequences of those choices. We often think of these as rewards or punishments, but many consequences are simply facts we must live with rather than moral judgments or treats for good behavior. Small choices add up. The sum of the consequences of our actions is what shapes our world.

JANUARY 22
Leave footprints

Wherever you walk, you leave footprints for others to follow, guiding them through. You are a part of history and the cycles of the world. You can be bold and inspire others. Look to create the world that you would want those in the future to be born into. While you are only one person, you are capable of creating great change, not just through your own actions but also through the actions you spark in others.

JANUARY 23
Achievements come in all shapes

What you achieve in your life is not just the sum of awards and promotions, congratulations and trophies. Your smallest acts of kindness reverberate through the world; that is an achievement in and of itself. What you do on a small scale, how you treat other people in times of stress and difficulty, are achievements that can have far more impact than any specific goal you work toward. To help the world thrive and become better is a beautiful, important achievement that lives on long after you.

JANUARY 24
Memory has power

Whether they fade gently with time or retain the sharpness of the present as the years go by, your memories are a precious part of who you are. How you remember the world shapes the present you live in, and shapes the future you create for yourself. Memory crafts our self-conception, anchors us in the narrative of our life, and creates shared bonds with others.

JANUARY 25
Life comes in cycles

Cycles are portals through which we step into the future. They cannot be stopped as they turn through time, taking us with them, only appreciated for the value they bring into our lives. We cannot appreciate ease without a measure of difficulty, nor do we truly understand our luck until it runs out occasionally. As the wheel of the year turns, it takes us through the natural rhythm of the seasons and allows us to depend on what comes next.

JANUARY 26
Release stress

Each of us experiences periods of stress and worry. To untangle the thread of our anxieties is real and meaningful work, and learning to process them is an education in itself. The world can be a stressful place, broken and difficult to deal with. You do not have to solve every problem to alleviate your stressors, but you do need to put in place ways of coping and building your resilience. It's a part of being healthy, a form of self-care to treat yourself kindly and find strategies for gentleness.

JANUARY 27
Let the universe make its own plans

We can make our plans, and yet the universe makes its own plans, takes its own paths. It's impossible to predict how the world will shape the plans you lay, and how it may surprise you. An openness to the twists and turns your plans may take is an openness to the mystery of the universe. Can you allow the plans you make to surprise you?

JANUARY 28
Work together

The role we play in this world lies at the center of a network of obligations, rights, and privileges we hold in our hands. To live in community is to agree to negotiate the balance of these things together, and sometimes compromise for the greater good. Community is not all burdens and demands on our individuality; it helps us thrive as individuals to have the support of one another. We achieve incredible things when we work together, as long as we operate with care and respect.

JANUARY 29
It's okay to feel lost

The world is very large and complicated, isn't it? We are imperfect and often find ourselves winding around in the spaces we create for ourselves. It is easy to feel aimless and untethered in the bigness of the world. Your hands are for reaching. Your feet are for walking. The path may not be straight, but it is in front of you always.

JANUARY 30
Delays happen

Waiting is hard, especially when plans are laid and deferred. Uncertainty is difficult to deal with, ambiguous and strange to navigate. It is not too much to ask for things to happen when you plan them, but asking does not ensure it will be so. Learn to dwell gently in the uncertainty, to appreciate the way anticipation heightens your senses and your pleasures. What is meant to happen will happen, and you cannot rush it. Flexibility will be your best guide.

JANUARY 31
Persistence has its own rewards

Our urgency often makes us feel that the journey toward
our goals should be a straight line, that hard work should
immediately result in our gain. But the one road through
difficulty is meant to help us learn, help us discover our
truer purpose and desires. Persistence through trials
can be valuable, even though in the moment it often feels
meaningless. Learning from setbacks, or at the least
pushing through them into something new, gives us the
gift of resilience. It teaches us how durable and strong
we are in the face of struggle. You are much stronger
than you realize.

February

FEBRUARY 1
Create calm

You do not have to wait for a calm moment to chase a sense of peace in your life. Life is rarely easy, and it rarely offers calm moments that you have not carved out with intention and deliberation. Hold close the moments that soothe you, and look for ways to cultivate that calm on demand. It's a state of mind and an active practice; it will not arrive wrapped as a gift dropped into your lap. Think of it as a garden that needs your careful attention—get to planting, and you'll have somewhere beautiful to relax when you need it. All it takes is figuring out how to make it grow.

FEBRUARY 2
Ice has its own beauty

The cold has its own beauty, frosted to the edges, clear and delicate. The sharpness of ice can cut and cause otherwise solid objects to shatter. Despite its bite, the ice will melt. The sun will thaw and it will transform into softness and fluidity. It will water the grass, nurture the ground, help usher in the green of spring. For now, it sparkles, and we wait for the world to turn toward warmth again.

FEBRUARY 3
Hibernation is valuable

The pleasure of being wrapped in warmth with no particular place to go and no agenda to pursue—when was the last time you allowed yourself to hibernate? Winter can feel endless, but when it's over, the hustle of spring's busyness rushes you forward into action. For now, be still. Allow yourself the comfort of a slow world, a warm home, and the joy of a sense of endless time. Do not rush the turning of the season; your hibernation will end soon enough in the sun.

FEBRUARY 4
It's all a journey

It is a long way to your destination, so you might as well enjoy the winding road that takes you there. It will take you to many unexpected places, and you will find many of them uncomfortable or less than joyful. But there will also be moments of unexpected delight that bring you joy you never anticipated. You cannot have one without the other, and to have them all you must set one foot in front of the other, taking the steps to begin your journey toward something new.

FEBRUARY 5
Apologies show growth

How often we are wrong, and yet how difficult it can be to admit it. Of course, no one is right all the time. We know this, and yet when it is our turn to face our mistakes, the embarrassment, the shame, and the regret color our view and drag at our pride. Very few things are black and white, and even mistakes we regret deeply have lessons to teach us about ourselves and others. Don't be afraid to own your mistakes, and to learn from them.

FEBRUARY 6
Moods are temporary

The sky is a constant, despite its changing moods. While it shifts in color, the sky is always the same above us, the lens through which we view the universe. You too have your moods that color your view, dramatic shifts of light and dark, colors that splash over how you see the world and wash your perception in shades and tones. Your anger and your joy are as changeable as the clouds and as dramatic as the sunset, and they fade with the same regularity. The person you are underneath remains, stable and unchanged by the shifting view.

FEBRUARY 7
Acceptance is its own strength

There are things in this world you cannot change; the hours pass without pause, the sun sets and rises without your permission. The seasons change and roll forward in a rhythm all their own. The past rolls back behind us, and our experiences there cannot be changed. What is in your power is your own actions, your interactions with others, and the choices you make as you move forward. Do your best to make sure these things align with your values, and don't be afraid to change when you learn something new. Be bold in your choices. Assess what is changeable, and leave what is not.

FEBRUARY 8
Comfort is coming

We all seek comfort in different ways; through companionship and caring for others, through time alone to think. Our creative powers and our inspiration help us find solace in each other, in art, and in time spent processing our emotions. There is no comfort like time, which soothes all wounds and all ails. Do what you can to get through the moment, and know that every difficulty is temporary. Comfort is coming.

FEBRUARY 9
Listen for what you hear in silence

You might not be able to hear it at this moment, but the world is still busy. It is right on schedule, and so are you. Each of us has a quiet period, or many quiet periods, if we are lucky. The world is doing exactly what it should be doing in its silence, and so are you. If you cannot hear what you are supposed to be doing, it is exactly this, in this moment, in this quiet.

FEBRUARY 10
Your heart will warm again

Heaving and sighing, the ground is slowly thawing in the lengthening days. The end of winter does not come quickly. The melt happens on its own schedule, in fits and starts. Do not fear if the winter appears again, and ice shows up to ruin the fun. It will pass, and your heart will warm with it. Get ready to grow again, and stretch your limbs in the sun.

FEBRUARY 11
Seeds need time to germinate

The seeds you have planted in the previous seasons are almost ready to emerge. The time they spent in the ground, waiting, was not wasted. Every single plan and plant needs its own time to germinate, to weigh the warmth and light until conditions are just right to thrust forth new life. Your hopes are germinating too, waiting for their own time to thrive. Everything blooms on its own schedule, and your plans are no exception.

FEBRUARY 12
Prune old growth

What no longer serves the larger purpose of your life? As you refine your goals and hone your direction, you'll realize that not every path is worth wandering down. Don't be afraid to prune back the habits and parts of yourself that interfere with the direction in which you are attempting to grow. What remains will be strong and intentional, ready to be a foundation for new growth and blooms.

FEBRUARY 13
Build trust

Trust is a bridge between the current moment and a million possibilities, between you and other people. It must be earned, built brick by brick, each choice creates a bond that holds fast. Like any bridge, it requires maintenance, attention, and investment. It can be dismantled in a flash, or slowly by erosion. It can be swept away in a flood. But it can be rebuilt, if you are willing to put in the work. Trust can hold you together in the torrents of life as well, and bring clarity, joy, and stability in a world full of floods and torrents.

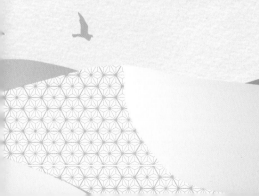

FEBRUARY 14
Every year allows rebirth

Every winter, no matter how long and cold, fades into warmth eventually. The cycle of life has its ebbs and flows, full of death and rebirth. When the world emerges in the spring, we all take part. It's not just the flowers that bloom. Our hearts and bodies flourish in the gentle warmth of the changing seasons. Though it will eventually grow hot and even harsh, we welcome the turn of the world and the changing of the seasons as a journey we take together. The change keeps the world alive, and us with it.

FEBRUARY 15
You are cherished

You do not have to prove your love or your value to the world. Love is not earned; it is there for you to hold in your hands and in your heart. Who holds your heart for you, reaches out hands to hold you? You deserve to be cherished and warmed by the love all around you. You are precious to the universe, utterly unique and individual. Let yourself be loved by those who would embrace you.

FEBRUARY 16
Be vulnerable

Sharing yourself with others is not easy; it can even be painful. It's not something that everyone is capable of, to give to other people what we'd usually keep for ourselves. Exposing our flaws and anxieties is a difficult process, and we can only hope that others will return their own vulnerability in exchange. To be vulnerable is, however, incredibly brave, and something to be proud of even when it is not returned. Do not let anyone make you feel ashamed of your ability to be vulnerable—vulnerability is a superpower.

FEBRUARY 17
The darker the sky, the brighter the stars

For you to see the stars, the sun must take its rest and be quiet. The night has its own time to shine, richly decorated in its own way. When the carpet of stars rolls out across the sky, we don't ask it to be as bright as day. The stars have their own charms, ones we can only appreciate when we're in the dark. The darker the sky, the brighter the stars shine, the more we can enjoy these dots of precious joy across the heavens.

FEBRUARY 18
Hope

Hope is beautiful, terribly fragile, and wildly powerful. It can overcome so much: pain, suffering, obstacles so large we cannot face them alone. Together our hope can be a force for good in the world, help us envision a better and more just existence for all of us. It can also merge the important parts of reality that we need to face. Balance your hope with your actions. Hope alone cannot dismantle the problems of the world, but it can push you forward into a new commitment to creating a better future.

FEBRUARY 19
You can always do better

Every day is a chance to do better, and be better.
You can step forward into a new day with all the
knowledge of the past, and make new choices. The goal
is not perfection, just improvement. You don't need to
seek others' approval to be better; only you can act in
ways that prove you are learning from the past. Compare
your present self only to your past. Move forward, and let
go of what you have done in the past. Your mistakes will
not disappear, but you can rise above them.

FEBRUARY 20
Forgiveness is an exchange

You cannot force forgiveness—not forgiveness from
others, and not forgiveness from yourself. Sometimes
the hurt of not being forgiven is a necessary pain, for
learning and for growing. Other times, an inability to
forgive others or ourselves takes up space in our hearts,
eats away at our joy and tenderness. Can you give
yourself the space to do better? Can you grant yourself
the freedom and closure of releasing old hurts that
occupy your spirit? Ultimately, the only person who can
give you forgiveness is yourself.

FEBRUARY 21
Celebrate the sunrise

In the morning, the sun will rise. There is no question of whether it will or not. The earth turns as we sleep, moving us closer to a new day. The spinning world greets the day with a burst of color, heralding new opportunities and potential joys. The sunrise is a celebration of this new and regular beginning. It is no less miraculous for the fact that it comes every morning. Celebrate with the sun, and start your day with a party.

FEBRUARY 22
Respect the earth

Every living thing in the world is deserving of respect.
In fact, even the nonliving elements of the environment
deserve respect. The mountains and the sea have been
here far longer than you, and will continue long after
you're gone. The trees breathe so you can breathe.
You are part of something so much larger than yourself,
this living world full of mysteries we are just beginning to
understand. You do not have to understand perfectly
to understand that it is precious.

FEBRUARY 23
Let the water come

Splash! That's the sound of the earth coming alive under your feet, rain collecting to nourish what's waiting to emerge. With every hour, the sun shines more, and the days grow longer. Can you feel it, the slow recession of the winter cold? There may still be a chill, even ice. It may be hard to believe that spring is on its way, but it's coming in its own sweet time, rushing ahead of you.

FEBRUARY 24
Sing

Raise your voice and sing. You do not need to be a songbird to join in the chorus of the day. Singing is not just for performance; it is also for expression and release. Let yourself be loud; take up space with your voice without fear or judgment. Your voice is precious and unique, connected to your spirit. It can liberate you, free you from your cares and anxieties, create joy, or express sadness. It does not matter what you sound like, only that you are heard.

FEBRUARY 25
The flowers are waiting

In autumn, hardy bulbs are set out in the soft soil to wait patiently through the freeze. They endure the cold, the snowfall, and the heaving ground in order to be the first ones in line to greet the sun and the spring. The moment the world is warm enough, they erupt in bloom, flying colorful flags of enthusiasm. Their patience is rewarded by our appreciation and excitement. The first flowers of spring are joy incarnate, a splash of color in the cold ground not yet thawed.

FEBRUARY 26
Breath is a constant thing

Our breath is a constant thing, with us whether we pay it any mind or, more often, forget about breathing entirely. It doesn't require our constant attention, but flows from moment to moment, keeping us afloat. And it is always there for us, giving us a path through the moment. In and out, any moment, any feeling, any event, your breath finds a way.

FEBRUARY 27
Look for the rainbow

The rain washes away many things, and brings life with it. As it falls, it nourishes a waiting earth. Rain is associated with gray and gloom, but the rainstorm is full of beauty, too. When the sun emerges from behind the clouds, it paints the sky with color and luck. Look for the rainbow that comes after the rain. Watch how the sun shines through its prism, and let the ways in which the sky can surprise you bring you joy.

FEBRUARY 28/29
Stretch

As spring approaches and the world begins to warm,
pay attention to the way life around you rises to the
occasion. The plants are waiting, full of potential energy
and anticipation. They will uncoil and grow, stretching
themselves to greet the sun. They are preparing even if
you cannot see them yet. They will climb and cover the
whole world with green when the time comes.

March

MARCH 1
Awaken to a new day

When the world rubs its eyes and wakes from sleep, it stirs every creature. The days grow long with light, and the windows open, airing out the staleness of cold. It may waver, but eventually the world tips into wakefulness and activity, humming a morning song. The waking up to new things cannot be rushed, but only planned for and anticipated. Let the sweetness of the morning of the world bring you along with it, waking up your joy and your optimism as it grows.

MARCH 2
Step into the light

A room full of darkness, and then suddenly, a flicker lights the gloom. All you need for a moment of clarity is a moment of illumination. Can you strike a match in the darkness for yourself? If you can create a moment of light for yourself, you might be able to build more light and light the candles of others, creating moments of clarity that build on themselves. Your light can help dispel any gloom; all it takes is your faith in its powerful glow.

MARCH 3
Life is a cycle

The world spins and spins, creating cycles of seasons that we rely on. Our life moves in cycles too, births and deaths, good and bad. We grow and learn, constantly returning to moments of stillness and renewal. This is not to say the process is always easy; after all, night follows day, rest follows work, joy follows pain. But the wheel keeps turning, proving all things are impermanent, especially our moments of difficulty.

MARCH 4
Things will change

A new world is possible with every choice you make. Will you welcome the new and its change? It comes after the cold and the dark, but it is not always comfortable. It will challenge you to become something different, and better than you were. A breath of fresh air, joyful and sweet, sweeping in across warming days: that's what a change of pace can do. To step into a new existence is not easy, but if the world can move through cycles of growth and stillness and growth again, so can you.

MARCH 5
Your plans are seeds you plant

Every action we take plants the seeds of future actions and future ideas. When you make a choice, when you think through a problem or goal, these actions will yield unexpected fruits. Unpredictable and wild, the seeds of our thoughts, actions, and choices feed our soul and begin the process of growing the future. Do not be afraid to plant your own seeds and make your own choices. Let them grow into a future that cannot be contained.

MARCH 6
Your rituals have power

The days have a rhythm, full of unconscious rituals we create for ourselves. Waking, washing, coffee, a walk—it is easy to take these things for granted as individual moments of repetition. But they are also an opportunity to create intentional rituals to bolster your heart and reinforce your spirit. As you go through your day, can you wake up to these moments of ritual? The more deliberate you can be, the more meaningful they will become.

MARCH 7
Faith will guide you

Belief is stronger than the confines of difficulty and hardship. Having faith in something deeper and higher than yourself can help you find your strength, even if what you believe in is the future. The future needs you to build it. Let it call to you, and let it make you strong. No matter what happens, it is coming, and you can make it better than the present. Have faith in yourself and what is coming.

MARCH 8
Encourage gentleness

Our world celebrates toughness, roughness, and a thick skin. It is easier to live in the world with such things. Our hearts break over and over again, and even this process makes us feel that gentleness is weakness. Your gentleness is a source of so much power, and it is so needed. Tenderness allows us to reach out to others, build connections, draw strength from each other. It helps us forgive, and it helps us love. Don't relinquish your gentleness.

MARCH 9
Every moment has possibility

A million paths lie in front of you. You can make whatever choice feels right. It does not have to look like your previous choices. You can be someone new; you can be the same person you were. It is entirely up to you. You may not be able to control the circumstances of where you make the choice or what, but the paths are there, waiting for you. They will lead you to new places, and you do not have to know where they will lead to make your choice.

MARCH 10
The cycle continues

The days lengthen and thaw, spreading green growth across empty ground. The flowers bloom and nod, turning to seed in their time. Seeds wait underfoot for the right moment to chill and then grow, bursting into the sun with fresh leaves. Our own lives have cycles of quiet and bloom too. A flower cannot grow indefinitely, or there would be no seeds of something new. Your life will move through the rhythms with the world, keeping its own time. You will grow, too.

MARCH 11
The thaw will come

Every icicle melts, every snowbank shrinks, every inch of ground softens in the thaw of spring. Making it past the frozen cold into something new, something rich with possibilities and freshness, takes patience. It takes faith in the cycles that bring us freeze and thaw, growth and rest. We cannot have one without the other, but it's okay to celebrate the release and the warmth. Let yourself dream of a gentler world, ready for planting with new seeds.

MARCH 12
Shift with the clouds

The sky is constantly moving and changing with the ebb of darkness and the coming or fading light. The blue is a constantly shifting hue dependent on the mood of the world and its timing. No matter what the mood, the clouds drift across the sky, not separate, but interlinked and responsive. They are sometimes full of bluster, or soft as down. They contain the wrath of storms and the gentle rain. Let yourself be as flexible and as ever-shifting as the clouds, with permission to change with the weather.

MARCH 13
Embrace repetition

Our days are filled with repetition, small moves repeated across time. While we pay the least attention to the way we pour our coffee and the way we make our bed (or not), these form the substance of our lives, making it possible for us to make the bigger moves and bigger decisions. We cannot exist without the daily routines that keep our lives running and that prove the foundation of larger selves. Make sure you give them a little attention today.

MARCH 14
Find your purpose

Not everyone believes in a higher power or specific deity, but everyone deserves to search for something higher than themselves. Believing in bigger concepts and bigger missions, the obligations of our communities and what we are to each other, can be our higher faith if we so choose. Alone, without a purpose, we are bound to wander and want, never feeling fulfilled or called. What is it that calls you forward into your life?

MARCH 15
Change happens

The world is not a stable place. It is a constantly changing cycle of life and death and rebirth. The seasons roll forward, changing all the time. Every choice unfolds the future with consequences and unforeseen impacts. This is not dire, but a joy. The instability is the space we need to change and improve, to learn and become better. There is no improvement without change, and no change without a little wobble to the world.

MARCH 16
Your senses can help you travel

Inhale deeply. What do you smell? Perhaps at first your brain will tell you that you smell nothing in this place where you are. But all around you is the scent of life, and you can focus on that and call it to you. Scent is a powerful call to memory. It can retrieve long-buried memories. It can encode feelings into the moment, so that this scent in this moment will bring you back here and now whenever you encounter it again.

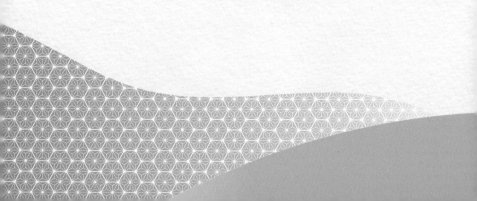

MARCH 17
Let yourself soften

Sometimes, in quiet moments, it is enough to feel the warmth, and let us warm our hearts as well as our bodies. Whether from a flame or something a little less primal, the warmth of our spaces and our loved ones is a gift worth valuing. How easy it is to take for granted the softness and the joy! But when you come in from the cold, tired and bedraggled, we remember how sweet the warmth of home and family can be.

MARCH 18
Stay in the moment

You are here! Look at you, breathing and growing in the miracle of the present moment! It is often said that every moment is a gift, but it is difficult to take account of each moment as it passes. We often long for them to be shorter or longer, to pass quickly or extend forever, but how can you collect the next gift if you insist on holding on to what you have? The future is an infinite string of these presents; all you have to do is open your hands and heart to receive them.

MARCH 19
Think about your desire

Want is a tricky thing, changeable and fleeting. What we want today may shift in the morning. As we learn and grow, what we want can transform, or even disappear. Does what your heart desires stand up to long-term investment? It's worth thinking carefully about what you want to sort out impulsive desires from the true messages of your heart. As the world spins and a new day dawns, let yourself shed what won't serve your success.

MARCH 20
Stretch beyond your limits

You will never know how far you can go if you do not stretch beyond the limit of what you think you are capable of. Even plants know this, reaching tendrils, vines, and leaves toward the light, ignoring the comfortable bounds of their pots. You are just as capable as any rose bush or ivy to reach, to climb, to overtake what you desire and move beyond the confines of comfort and imagination. Stretch out your hands, and grow.

MARCH 21
Accept your flaws

It is a tricky thing to accept our flaws. On the one hand, we know we should love ourselves despite the ways we might fall short. Perfection is just an ideal, and one we will never reach. On the other, it hurts to miss the mark, worrying our hearts that we may never measure up to the person we hope to be and the expectations of the people we love. To reconcile this tension, we must simultaneously accept who we are in this moment and still strive toward being better. This is the work of being human!

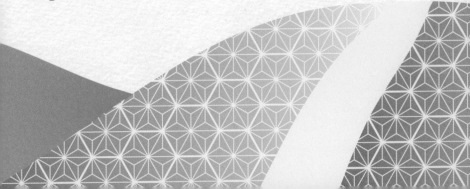

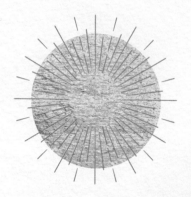

MARCH 22
Spark excitement

The racing of your heart, the thrill of something new: excitement is one of the most enriching parts of our experience. Excitement isn't always positive—after all, the fight-or-flight response is exciting, prompting a cascade of emotions and neurotransmitters, moving us to action. We profoundly associate excitement with joy and novelty. Let yourself be excited by things large and small! Negotiate a space between enjoying the anticipation and keeping your heart protected from the occasional disappointment.

MARCH 23
Love is all around

The world is rich in love, one of our few ever-renewing resources, flowing out from each of us to fill our hearts and build a better world. You too are surrounded by so much love. There are people in your life who will love you continually, no matter what happens or what mistakes you make. This kind of unconditional love helps us be better, change the world, and pass that love on to those who need it. Make sure to tell the people who give you this love how much they mean to you, and how much you love them in return.

MARCH 24
Discomfort is temporary

We all must deal with our fair share of discomfort in our lives, as passing as a stone in our shoe or as lasting as regret or grief. It is easy to forget that even discomfort ebbs and flows, changes with time. It is subject to the same forces as our memories. Time allows us to create space apart from discomfort to process and learn from it. How difficult this is to remember in the moment when we are experiencing discomfort! When you find yourself in such a moment, remember that it is temporary. Focus on what you can learn.

MARCH 25
There is freedom in failure

At some point, every single one of us falls short of
the goals and ideals we set for ourselves. Failure is
entirely normal, and human! Can you escape from the
expectations you set? You do not need to be perfect to
be worthy of love, care, and dignity. In fact, as you fail, you
are freer than you have ever been. Every moment is pure
potential, as you make choices about how you react and
where you go from here. Using what you learn, you can
make new choices. The paths in front of you are infinite—
where will you go?

MARCH 26
Release

Let go of what you think you should be, or ought to be.
Who are you right now, in this moment? You are carrying
around the weight of so many previous selves and
previous choices. It is not possible to go back and change
what has already happened. You can only move forward.
Drop the heavy load of regrets, and take with you only the
lessons you have learned. You are capable of so much joy,
and so much change. What you let go of will make space
for these things, and so much more.

MARCH 27
Compromise

You cannot always have what you want. You know that, of course, but the ability to negotiate the space between what you want and what others want is a specific skill, acquired only with practice. There are some things that you simply cannot compromise on, and that's okay. Know that holding fast to what you want can cost you. When you make this determination, you'll have to calculate: Is what you are holding on to worth what you might lose by not compromising? Don't give it all away, but it's important to ask yourself each time.

MARCH 28
Move on

Take that step forward. You are ready to embrace something new, and you cannot do it while dwelling in the past. You'll have to let go of many things to move forward, because the future needs your hands to be empty if it is to fill them with new opportunities. Moving on is a process of making space for the new while honoring the lessons of what came before it. What do you need to let go of to make this space for yourself?

MARCH 29
The frost will thaw

Even when the world thaws with warm sun and longer days, frost can sneak up on what's blooming and steal the process of spring. Seeds we planted and sprouts we watched carefully wilt under this icy touch. Setbacks are a part of life, and a natural part of the cycle of spring (and of life). What is meant to bloom will bloom at the right time. That goes for people as well as plants.

MARCH 30
Be ready

It's time to get ready. Ready for what, you ask? Ready for the rest of your life, which is coming fast. You will never know what opportunities are headed toward you, what mistakes you will need to recover from, and what joys lie waiting for you. The world is unpredictable and strange, but you can prepare your heart with openness for what's coming. You do not need to know what is in store, only to commit to as much grace as possible when it rises to meet you.

MARCH 31
Believe in miracles

Do you believe that miracles exist? You yourself are a miracle, one in a million billion possibilities. Each of us is a miracle in our own way, and every moment we draw breath and live together is an incredible gift. In all the vastness of the universe, here we are together in this moment. The connection between each of us is wildly unlikely, insanely improbable. How lucky we are to be together here, on this planet, at this moment.

April

APRIL 1
Growth can be challenging

It is not always easy to expand beyond your current shape and push out into new territory. Growth does not happen in the ways we expect, or in the directions we foresee. You're growing right now; can you feel it? Allow your ability to grow to surprise you with its scope and power. You have the ability to shape-shift, to leave behind old ways of being and seeing, and step into a new form. Every flower that blooms and tree that reaches to the sky starts as a seed, a sprout, something small, tender, and unassuming. The process requires only time and a willingness to become something new.

APRIL 2
Connect to others

The connection that we build with other people is what sustains us as a collective and individually. We owe each other care and attention, and need each other to sustain our hearts. How we reach out to one another and build connections moment by moment has the potential to transform our lives, wrapping us in a net of support and love. How can you reinforce your bonds with others, and strengthen your heart in the process?

APRIL 3
Be patient

Waiting isn't easy. It's simple to say that patience is a virtue, but much harder to keep patience in your life. There are many things we wait on: change, our hopes and dreams, our plans, our own readiness. Things come in their own time and cannot be rushed. You cannot make time go faster, or hasten the process.

APRIL 4
Positivity is powerful

There are two kinds of positivity in the world: one that conceals the truth of the matter, and one that understands that there are two sides to every coin. True positivity requires an acknowledgment of difficulty, the dark side of the coin, even as it searches for the shiny side. Let the coin spin, and see both sides. Choose to make the world better than it is, as good as its potential.

APRIL 5
Feel the rain

A rainy day is shorthand for a boring or hard day, but the rain is what feeds us all. It waters the plants, gives life to the animals around us, washes away the old, and invites new growth. Rain is a gift, part of the endless cycle of rebirth that the world around us dances through every season. Without it, we would wander lost and hungry, parched. When it rains, celebrate the joy of water and the cycles we are a part of.

APRIL 6
Let the fresh air in

Throw open the windows of your heart and let the breeze of a new season sweep through. Sometimes all we need is a brisk reminder that change is possible to freshen our outlook. It is so easy to get stuck in the same mind-set, the same set of expectations and desires, but the world is full of newness. The wind carries all sorts of potential. You can let it blow through you and change you, but you'll have to open the windows and doors first.

APRIL 7
Relish the anticipation

The moment of anticipation doesn't have to be a test of your patience. What if, instead, it was a long process that builds joy? Anticipation can heighten your appreciation if you let it. Allow the waiting to increase your gratitude for what is long awaited. Think of it as an opportunity to choose joy. Each moment draws it closer, allowing you to dwell in possibility. It's a process full of potential, generating its own energy. Allow it to fill you.

APRIL 8
Cycles are an anchor

We use the seasons as metaphors so often that the vast importance of them wears out. The importance of the cycle of our environment is not just a convenient aphorism. It is a cycle that feeds us, gives us water, clothes our bodies, and gives us the resources to grow, learn, and create joyful, meaningful experiences. Your favorite sweater was grown under the sun as a plant, or maybe started as grass that fed a wooly sheep. Think back to the deep origin of the things you touch and feel. Each person and thing are part of the cycle of seasons, however distant we imagine our modern lives being from nature.

APRIL 9
Fertilize your future

Without planting seeds, you cannot have the sweet fruit that ripens. Seeds are full of potential energy, but we cannot taste their sweetness without working with the forces around us. Every seed needs the help of others—the sun, the water, the soil, all feeding it to help it grow. It needs time and the patience of the planter. Every plan you lay and every dream you dwell in needs community and time as well. What are you planting, and what will it yield?

APRIL 10
Be a leaf

A paper-thin leaf powers the growth of trees that tower over us. How can something so small be so powerful? A leaf breathes, it grows and changes, it synthesizes all the energy a tree needs. Together with a community of leaves decorating the outstretched branches, a leaf helps send roots deep into the earth, sharing the energy, creating food and sweetness. If something so small can do so much by joining with others, imagine what you can achieve if you do the same.

APRIL 11
Rain is a gift

We talk about rain as a dreary thing, gray skies and full clouds blocking out the sun. But water gives us life, sends vital moisture into the soil and into the rivers, softening the ground and growing the plants. It grows our food, makes up the majority of our physical form, cleans off the sweat from our bodies. We are so dependent on water, and here it is, falling out of the sky toward our waiting world. The next time you see a raindrop, you might want to say thank you.

APRIL 12
Energy is everywhere

If you can feel your heart beating, you can feel energy. It's not mystical; it's not magic. Your heartbeat is as electric as a lightning bolt and as powerful as a thunderstorm. The energy of the world is all around you, waiting for you to tap into it. Love is energy, movement is energy, food is energy. It's all the same source, what moves between us all. Don't shut it out—reach out and touch the power of the universe.

APRIL 13
Everything is possible

You can change the world at any time. It's all a matter of choices, and of scale. A single call to a friend in need can change their day, change their life. A donation of time or money can alter the course of someone's fate for the better. A gift given freely can free someone from despair. The world is full of possibilities, and your choices shape them. What choices can you make today that will shift your sense of possibility?

APRIL 14
You are in a cocoon

You are waiting to become something greater and more beautiful than you are now. The process will require that you shed your old form to become this new thing, stripping you back to the essentials, rebuilding you as something entirely new. Can you imagine what you will become? You will fly far, beyond your wildest dreams, but first you must rest here in the dark, changing and shifting, a total metamorphosis.

APRIL 15
Everything begins with the same building blocks

Imagine the smallest thing you can. A pin, a mote of dust. Can you imagine its many molecules, its tiny atomic building blocks? If you can, go deeper, go smaller. Imagine its protons and electrons, whirling and linking, so much space between them that they twirl and dance easily. A million billion trillion tiny pieces, interlocking into objects as solid as a mountain and as delicate as a feather. When you reach out and touch, can you still see those tiny particles, how they blend at the tip of your finger into what you touch?

APRIL 16
Mixed success is still valuable

We like to separate success and failure into neat categories, piles of victory and defeat. But reality is not so simple and straightforward. Often our successes come with regrets, and our failures with a measure of celebration. Things are rarely tidy and clear. It's okay to complicate the process of completion. Nearly everything we experience in life is a mixture of many things, and you do not have to simplify your feelings to draw meaning from your experiences.

APRIL 17
Everything can be a ritual

Rituals are a powerful way to focus ourselves. We often engage in ritual without realizing we are doing so, but a ritual is just a routine that we endow with importance and meaning through our intention. By bringing your intention and attention to bear on any ordinary routine, you can turn it into a ritual of care. Even folding your laundry can be a ritual if you take it moment by moment, not wishing you were somewhere else, but instead reflecting on how wonderful what you have is, and how grateful you are for it.

APRIL 18
Don't stop searching

It is only natural to go looking for the next thing,
restlessly searching for an answer or a path. It's part
of being human, always on the lookout for something to
guide us. Don't feel like you have to solve the riddles of
the universe by yourself. Just because you are searching
doesn't mean you are lost. We are on a journey each of us
must undertake for ourselves, to discover the long path
of our life stretched out before us, leading us to
our purpose.

APRIL 19
Boredom can be good

While the saying goes that only boring people get bored,
the truth is that a little boredom is good for our brains.
When we do not have a mission or goal to occupy our
brain, it is then that we have space to reflect, process,
and reinvent. Don't be afraid to leave some hours
unoccupied. Let your mind drift and your soul dream.

APRIL 20
Disappointment happens

It's okay to fall short of what you imagined for yourself.
If someone has not told you this before, let yourself
believe it now. It does not mean that you are unworthy
of your goals, or that you should not try again. Each of
us must learn to build our resilience and our persistence.
There is no way to do so without choosing to push
through difficulty. Take your disappointments as lessons,
and move forward to try again with new knowledge.

APRIL 21
Adjustment is healthy

Not all discomforts are an obstacle, or even a bad thing.
We learn and grow by facing challenges, stretching
and adjusting all the time. An adjustment is not the
same thing as a compromise, exactly. A compromise
is a negotiation between two sets of boundaries or
desires. An adjustment is instead a necessary change of
attitude or position made with new knowledge in hand.
An adjustment need not be a sacrifice; it can be a gift to
both yourself and others. Can you tell the difference?

APRIL 22
It's time to thrive

Here they come! The new leaves and sprouts that herald the spring. They've been waiting for this moment, held inside buds and seeds, biding their time for the perfect moment so that they can thrive. Without rushing, in coordination with the sun and the cycles of the seasons, they emerge to color our world and fill it with life. Are you waiting for your perfect moment to thrive?

APRIL 23
Inspiration awaits

The world is calling to you with a million possibilities and ideas. Inspiration dances behind every bloom. You don't have to chase it. Instead, welcome it in. Set it a place at the table in your heart, and invite it to meet with you as your guest. How do you do that? Let yourself dream unoccupied, and let your hands dance over whatever makes your heart sing. When you find a thread that activates your curiosity, follow it, winding it as you go into something beautiful.

APRIL 24
Spring is coming

The air changes with the coming of spring, full of celebration and the scent of the new. Can you smell the leaves unfurling, the trees stretching their limbs? The birds know when it's spring, and so do you. Let it make your heart lighter. The smell of spring brings hope with it, the scent of the future and possibility. Anticipation of warmer days has its own sweetness.

APRIL 25
You can be better

You are worthy of love just as you are, but it doesn't mean you have to live a life in stasis. You can transform yourself into the kind of person you want to be. You can do better. You can be better than you are now. Who you want to be can change as well, shifting as you learn more about the world and yourself. Each choice is a chance to be someone new, and you do not need anyone's permission to do so.

APRIL 26
Let it be simple

Life is very complicated, often overwhelmingly so. Every day we are faced with thousands of choices, both large and small. We adapt as we learn, choosing differently as we learn more. But it can also be very simple. We can choose simplicity, choose to focus on life moment by moment. It is not always possible, but it is something we can cultivate. Right in this moment, what can you choose to let go of to make your life simpler?

APRIL 27
Greet the morning chorus

Your senses can help you connect with nature. Listen carefully as you wake in the morning. You do not have to jump directly into your day, diving into the news and your screens. Instead, tune in to the morning chorus of birds, welcoming you into a new day. Open the windows and welcome in the breeze and sun. The morning chorus was there long before we tuned into the hubbub of the world. Let yourself welcome the world unmediated by screens and chatter.

APRIL 28
Learn from mistakes

It can be painful to realize when you've made a mistake, especially if your mistake harms others. The only way to move forward is to allow the realization to shape and change how you act in the future. Your actions are the most important part of showing that you have learned and understood your mistakes. While you can ask others for forgiveness, you are only in charge of what you can do. What you can do is learn, and change.

APRIL 29
Flip your perspective

Dirt is often considered synonymous with negative things: a lack of cleanliness, a certain set of emotions like shame and failure. But dirt, or soil, is full of life—fungi and insects, nutrients and minerals. Dirt is a precious thing. It is the foundation of every part of our lives, growing our food, holding our homes in place, supporting our feet. Interrogate the part of you that associates dirt with specific concepts, and let yourself explore what it means to reconsider the fixed concepts around you.

APRIL 30
All living things are connected

The force that drives the green vine and the blooming flower, the force that pushes the growth of the seed into a sprout, this force also drives our hearts, pumps our blood, and expands our lungs. We are all connected by the constantly changing, shifting force of life that allows us to grow and change. While we can explain many things, that force is ultimately a mystery we dwell inside of, a complex tangle of consequences and interlocking existences. It is the shared inheritance of all life, plants and people alike.

May

MAY 1
Ride the momentum

The river rolls and rolls, picking up speed as it goes. Life feels the same way, picking up speed as we move through it, the years gaining momentum and weight. Sometimes the speed scares us; the moment is too swift for us. At other times, the swiftness feels like a dance, a course laid out for us to follow. You don't need to be afraid of the momentum. To move forward opens the way to growth and better things.

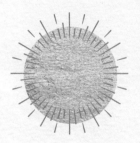

MAY 2
Embrace the sunrise

It pours and spills over the horizon, lighting up our days and bringing clarity. Whether the length of the day is waxing or waning through the year, the sun rises every morning to offer us a fresh start. As the day begins, it is a new chance to build again, to start something new. How will you use this opportunity? Set your intentions by the sun, and let each new morning renew your commitment to yourself.

MAY 3
Breathe

Inhale. You are in this moment, and capable of moving through it. Exhale. You are through the moment, and into the next. Your breath moves you forward, and here you are, moving through and forward. As your chest rises and falls, feel the space it creates. That space is always there, waiting for you. It holds your heart, and welcomes you. Your breath comes in and out with no effort. It can lead you through difficult or intense moments, a locus of focus for your mind to anchor your mind to your body. Its constancy can keep you company.

MAY 4
Be like the birds

We humans have always been slightly envious of birds, borrowing them as a symbol of freedom and peace. They fly across borders in long seasonal migrations that bring them home, uniting as a flock as they mark time in the sky. We borrow them for joy, too, with their songs that greet the day. Can you sing with the birds and greet the day as well?

MAY 5
Examine from every angle

We want simple answers. Solutions are most convenient when they are black and white. Looking for what is easy to spot, we toss aside nuance and complication in favor of what makes sense from where we are standing. It is much more difficult to spend time looking at the gray spaces between, and accept that there are many things that are true at once. When we give up simple answers, we can embrace the beautiful complexity of the world as it is, rather than the world as we would like to see it.

MAY 6
Be wild

You do not have to be tame to be loved and valued. Your wildness is valuable, too, the part of you that wishes for the freedom to run. It can take you far if you let it. Each of us tames ourselves in one form or another to make ourselves palatable. We fear being too wild for others. Can you look for and recognize the wildness in others? Accept the wildness in yourself, and you'll find the wildness in those around you is much less difficult to handle.

MAY 7
Go down the rabbit hole

Inspiration for how to live is all around us, in the life that thrives in every patch of green. There's so much life that you do not even see, dwelling below your feet. Imagine the rabbit in the field, munching on clover. When it sees you and disappears from view, it heads to the cozy world you cannot see, a network of burrows and tunnels, protected, warm, and safe. How can you make your home as welcoming as a rabbit's cozy abode?

MAY 8
The ground beneath your feet tells a story

The ground we walk on rarely gets our consideration. We cover it in asphalt and concrete, build on it and plant in it. What lies under our feet is in fact something very special, a blend of each and every life that has passed through it, stones that have seen a number of years we cannot even start to fathom.The mixture of tiny, microscopic lives, the tangle of mycelia and hair-thin roots, is full of living things, carrying on without us. No matter where you stand, if you go deep enough, that community is waiting.

MAY 9
You are allowed to rest

Rest is not earned; it is a necessity, as important to your body as water and air. We often feel that we must work in order to be ready for rest, but we can and should give our body as much rest as it needs. Leave aside productivity and laziness, and make space for these requirements. You do not have to fill every hour with busyness. Stretch your limbs and ease your tension. Relax your vigilance, and tend to your body with care.

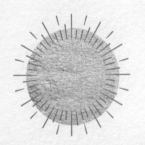

MAY 10
We owe each other

Our lives are not a separate thing, wound tightly around only ourselves. Instead, our actions and obligations are threads that bind us to one another. The life we live is part of innumerable other lives in ways big and small. From the people we know and love to the people we brush against in passing, what we owe one another within the ties that bind make us a community. We pursue a better world together, and do our best to treat each other with understanding, respect, and dignity.

MAY 11
Life has its tensions

Life does not always flow easily, and we do not always flow easily with one another. Misunderstandings, mistakes, and missed opportunities keep us from always communicating perfectly. With many different perspectives, we cannot always agree with one another. And occasionally one or both parties may simply be in the wrong. The tension that strained the bonds we have with one another must be sat with, processed, and acknowledged; otherwise, we cannot better understand each other, grow, or change. This truth helps us find moments of peace and process the tension that is bound to occur.

MAY 12
There are many paths

There are many paths we can take in life. Each choice opens as many roads as it closes. Your choices are always arrayed out in front of you, even when you cannot see them. Other people will make different choices for better or worse, but you will never have the exact same set of choices, nor can others walk the exact same paths as you. Your path is yours alone to choose and walk. Celebrate the paths you choose to take—no one else can walk them in quite the same way!

MAY 13
You can evolve

Evolution makes all things possible, from the beginning of life on this planet to the transformation of the spirit. The ability of living things to adapt and change is one of the great and wild gifts of the universe. You don't have to wait generations to transform yourself and the world. You can shed what isn't serving you right now, right here. You can choose change and make your moves, go from land to sea and back again. Go ahead, astound the world with your shape-shifting.

MAY 14
Soothe yourself

Each of us feels our own griefs and pains, and each of us needs ways to soothe ourselves. The sun can soothe a weary spirit, and rest can soothe a weary body. What are the ways that you can take care of both your spirit and your body? How can you support your nervous system and protect your tender heart? Taking care of yourself is as important as any other obligation you have to work or to others. You cannot give of yourself or to yourself if your cup is empty.

MAY 15
You are a part of everything

There is no such thing as a life apart from other lives.
Your life is a link in a chain that wraps around the whole
of the world. Every creature big and small is a part of it,
as is every plant. You could not exist if the bee did not
exist. The grass is as important as you are. It's a strange
lesson to learn that human beings are not inherently
more important than any other part of our worldwide
net of support and mutual dependence. But just think:
Everything that lives is your neighbor, your family,
your friend.

MAY 16
Try anyway

There is no shame in feeling unequal to the task at hand.
Sometimes all we can do is face our fears, and try our
hand anyway. Just because we don't always succeed does
not mean we should not attempt to stretch beyond our
limits. In fact, the world demands it. Each of us falls short
in some ways as we reach, but it is the reach that counts.
It is the only way to exceed our own limits, and stretch
toward the impossible dreams.

MAY 17
All it takes is a single drop

One drop is all it takes to create a ripple that extends far beyond the initial impact. The waves of the actions we take push out from the moment, creating change far beyond the locus of our actions. You cannot begin to imagine what effects your actions will create, so it is best to be as thoughtful as possible when you act. Once you do, release your action into the universe and hope that the ripples turn into the right kind of waves. All you can do is act, release, hope, and try again.

MAY 18
Offer forgiveness

Forgiveness is a curious thing; we need it from others, but we cannot control or compel it from others. We need it from ourselves too, but it is often just as hard to receive it. It is possible to move forward without forgiveness, and even sometimes necessary, but it is always easier and more healing to offer forgiveness when you can. That goes for the forgiveness you give yourself. Let yourself move forever, and offer that gift to yourself.

MAY 19
Mistakes happen

Are you afraid to admit a mistake? None of us is free
from error. Every single one of us makes mistakes, but to
ignore them or sidestep responsibility only compounds
the error. You are better than your mistakes, and capable
of doing better each time you try. Our ego tries to
protect us by telling us we cannot possibly be wrong, or
that the responsibility is not ours. Don't let pride get in
the way of your own learning and growth.

MAY 20
Let yourself be loved

You are so loved, even when you feel alone. All around you
the love of the world is radiating toward you. The love of
your family and friends is all around you. You belong to the
world, and deserve to be seen by others, fully and without
reservation. Your only job is to love as fully and completely
as you can in return.

MAY 21
Try to be good

You do not have to be good all the time. But goodness
is always worth striving for, no matter where you are in
your life. You deserve to be good to yourself, and you are
responsible for being good to others. You do not have to
be perfect, to be good every moment of the day. That's
too much pressure to put on yourself or others. You still
owe it to yourself and others to try.

MAY 22
Conflict can be creative

How do you find yourself reacting when conflict arises? Your response to the disagreements that inevitably occur gives you enormous insight into your mental state. Friction within relationships is inevitable—each person has a different experience, a different perspective that informs their point of view. The part that is within your control is how you navigate the situation, the choices you make, and the way you react. Focus on saying and doing what you can to minimize harm, and give grace to yourself and others whenever possible.

MAY 23
Embrace sweetness

There is an abundance of sweetness and tenderness in the world, waiting for you to embrace it. Sometimes it feels inaccessible, but it is always there. You can find it in the love of others, in the support and solidarity of your community, in the small pleasures that delight your heart. The natural world is full of beauty and sweetness, too, if you commit to spending time outside to see it. Every raindrop softens the earth, every sunbeam warms skin and stone. If you feel cut off from the flow of tenderness, try extending it to others, and see how the sweetness returns.

MAY 24
Transformation is possible

Would you believe that a caterpillar becomes a butterfly if no one had taught you about cocoons? This small earthbound thing that moves in inches turns into a dainty thing with wings, beautiful to behold, strong enough to cross continents. It has an entirely different shape, an entirely different character. The in between is a mess. It cannot be disturbed in the process, no peeking inside the cocoon to check if it's done. Transformation is a tricky business that cannot be rushed. Don't be afraid if your own transformation is a mess, too, unidentifiable while it becomes something beautiful, resilient, and unfamiliar.

MAY 25
Bloom like a wildflower

Sometimes, flowers bloom where you did not realize you planted seeds. They spring up to create beauty where you least expect it, an unanticipated gift from the past. What seeds in your life have you planted that have gone untended but still might bring beauty into your life? Everywhere you go, each act of kindness, every choice you make, leaves a trail of seeds, plans set in motion intentionally or not. They may yet bloom into beauty in your life!

MAY 26
Step to the edge

To be on the verge of a decision or change is like a
bird standing on the edge of a nest for the first time,
waiting to take flight. You know you have wings, but no
confident experience to be sure they will be able to carry
you. You do not know how far you will be able to travel.
All you can do is have faith. Jump, and trust your wings will
bring you where you are supposed to be.

MAY 27
Everything begins again

The darkness of winter is a time of hibernation and
reflection. What follows in the spring is a rebirth of sorts,
emerging from the quiet into light and sound to start
anew in the sun. When the world thaws and comes alive,
so can you. The world feels new. Flowers emerge from
bulbs, tall stalks reaching for the sun. Reach for a new way
of being in your body, and a new way of being in the sun.

MAY 28
Restlessness can guide you

How often we treat our restlessness as a sign of boredom when it is instead a sign of growth. It is necessary and appropriate that we should crave new challenges and new knowledge as we move through the world. It should not surprise or scare you—it does not mean there is something wrong or lacking. Let your restlessness lead you toward a new way of being without abandoning who you are. It's all part of the cycle.

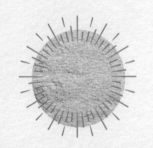

MAY 29
Flow like water

Water always finds a way to move, seeping through soil, cutting caverns and riverbeds into rock, sculpting with persistence. Even puddles move, evaporating into the air, falling back from the clouds to join the sea. Floods rage and gentle trickles seep into the sidewalk. Water always finds a way to move into the next moment to become something new. It is never static. It cannot be contained because it knows how very necessary it is to the movement of the world itself.

MAY 30
Unfurl

We hold ourselves so tightly to protect our hearts. The world can be cold and difficult, and so we stay close, protectively clenched in a defensive posture. Our hearts are like an unopened bud at the tip of a branch, waiting for the right moment to unfurl. The warmth and the growth are coming; it's okay to wait until you are ready. The leaves know what time is right to emerge, and so will you.

MAY 31
Beginnings are endings

It is often said that every ending contains a new beginning, but the beginnings flow everywhere you look, and endings, too. Every moment is a new chance to begin again, to do better, to do things differently. You do not have to be perfectly good, perfectly wise, perfectly planned to begin again.

June

JUNE 1
Trust the timing

The days lengthen, and the seeds you've planted have begun to grow. Hard work takes time to pay off, and often we cannot even see the results of our work until they surprise us. Trust that the work you are doing will yield its own rewards if you give your efforts the time they need to flourish. All you have to do is return to the work; be resilient and persistent, and flexible when necessary.

JUNE 2
Listen to your heart

Can you hear it? Your heart is always speaking to you, drumming out a message in bursts and pangs, a language you can feel as much as you can hear. At some points in your life, it will speak so loudly it cannot be ignored. Other times, it will lie quietly and you will have to listen very hard to hear it. The messages it brings will guide you and help you find your purpose. Listen to what it says.

JUNE 3
Start blooming

Have you been waiting to show your true colors? It requires time and patience to become something new, to shine in a new way. But you are blooming, beautiful and sweet. Your colors and patterns will attract new visitors and carry you beyond your garden walls. Your bloom adds beauty to the world, unique and precious. Treasure this moment and enjoy it and your blooming. Not everyone blooms at the same time, but we all bloom again and again, in our own seasons.

JUNE 4
Creativity comes in waves

The ebb and flow of your creativity can be an
unpredictable tide, but it's not a sea that can be tapped
dry. When you feel the tide of your creativity pulling away
from the shore, there's no need to chase it. The waves
will come back to shore, bringing new ideas and new
inspiration for you. You can force neither the rhythm of
the waves nor their speed, but if you stand on the shore,
creativity will come to greet you.

JUNE 5
Find your purpose

What are you searching for? Is it within your grasp, or so far away that you cannot imagine reaching out and touching it? If you are waiting until you have it to enjoy the world around you, ask yourself what you are missing out on. Is it possible you have everything you need in your hands already? You do not need to stop reaching, but consider what is already within your grasp that brings you joy and satisfaction.

JUNE 6
The sun is waiting

The warmth of the sun makes all things possible, waking the seeds in soil, calling plants and animals into the light. It calls you too, asking you to come outside and bask in the light. Grow toward the light like a vine, and embrace the possibility of abundance. The sun asks us to reach further, stretch higher, to bloom. It's all part of a cycle—the flowers turning to seed, the seeds resting in the cold, then waking in the warmth. Where are you in the cycle? Look for your sun, and reach.

JUNE 7
Feel how alive you are

Stretch your limbs and wiggle your toes. Circle your arms in your joints and roll your neck. Take a deep breath. Here you are, alive in the world! You are part of this world, a miracle of electrical currents and molecules and chemical reactions. Everything alive shares in this dance, this constant flow and ebb of life. What a miracle it is to join together in this whirl, part of everything and yet totally unique.

JUNE 8
Chase your dreams

What are you chasing right now? Your goals and ambitions are stretched out in front of you, waiting for you to seize them. The chase is long, and it's hard work. The road that leads you toward those precious end points is full of obstacles. You are strong and capable enough to face them. Keep up the chase, and don't stop until you've reached the finish line. Let your dreams carry you forward.

JUNE 9
You belong to the universe

Can you imagine where you stand, the point on the map?
Now zoom out, imagining the world hanging in space,
rotating in all its speed around the sun, the sun enormous
and warm. Go further, go wider, let the galaxy whirl
around in the vastness of space. Envision the innumerable
galaxies that keep it company, let them tumble through
the dark. How many can you make space for? Finite, small,
and brilliant, you belong in this enormous world, to this
enormous world.

JUNE 10
Every moment is an opportunity

All around you are opportunities to build and grow. It
only takes your outstretched hand to reach toward
them. We take for granted the resources at our disposal,
dismissing what is available to us as not enough, or too
common. But every moment is an opportunity. Each
person in your life is an untapped and vast source of
knowledge. What you have at your fingertips is more
valuable than you realize. Open your eyes to what is
already in your hands.

JUNE 11
Find the joy in failure

When you start from the ground, you can only go up. When you fail, you knock down whatever ladders you have built, and you can build again. Failure is a kind of clean slate. You should learn from what you have experienced, but in the moment of failure, you are also able to start over with that new knowledge. Try again! Try a new way. You are free to try and try again. Now, at the very least, you know what not to do.

JUNE 12
Inhale the smell of summer

A thousand blooms waving in the sun, warm grass under your feet, a kaleidoscope of color everywhere you look. The smell of summer is fragrant and unique, a welcoming spell cast on long days of sunshine. Whether to you summer means salty sea air or cool rivers and lakes, dust on the wind or humidity, summer is a period for embracing the length of the days and the warmth that envelops them.

JUNE 13
Listen to the thunderstorm

The crash and the thunder, the rolling storm and the flash of lightning: the thunderstorm is a fireworks show that the sky puts on for you. Thunder is not a threat; it is just the sound of heat confronting cold. Lightning is the same force that powers your heart—you have lightning inside you, too. Don't let the fury and the sound scare you. Remember, it's as much a part of you as your own skin and blood. Enjoy the show!

JUNE 14
Be authentic

Authenticity is not always beautiful or perfect.
To be authentic is to make mistakes and ask for
forgiveness. But authenticity also requires you to
shine, to glow brightly in your uniqueness. It requires
you to step into your own power with bravery, and use
that power to help others too. It is not always easy to
be authentic; in fact, it can often be quite hard. But it will
always be a better course of action to be authentically
flawed than inauthentically flawless.

JUNE 15
Release your expectations

Our hearts want so much, and expect so much from the
world. It is difficult to let go of our expectations of how
the world should be when it does not go according to our
plans. Can you release the weight of expectations that
have been placed upon you? You do not have to measure
up to someone else's plans to be worthy of love and care.
Others do not have to measure up either. You can only
try your best, and hope that it is enough to carry
you forward.

JUNE 16
Friendship is a celebration

One of the greatest joys in our lives is the relationships and connections we build with others. Friendship is the bedrock of our communities, crossing lines of identity and experience, knitting us together in a web of care. Your friendships can fill your heart and sustain your spirit. Make sure that you are giving your friends' hearts the same care and attention your own heart needs. Friendship is a two-way street, and the connections you build require maintenance and care just like any other bonds you have.

JUNE 17
Admit your mistakes

While we all make mistakes, it is difficult to admit when we are wrong. Our pride and our ego can get in the way. It hurts us to confront the ways in which we have fallen short, even if it is an unintentional mistake. The only way to remedy our mistakes is to acknowledge the error and attempt to make things right. Some things once broken cannot be repaired, but the vast majority of things can be fixed with a little care and honesty.

JUNE 18
The mirror is a tool

When you look in the mirror, what do you see? Do you meditate on your reflection and the person that you are, or do you immediately begin to look for flaws? The reflection in the glass is all light and color, as temporary as the moment it reflects back to you. The person in the mirror needs your love, your support, your protection and care. The person in the mirror is deserving of all the good that comes your way. Don't go searching for your flaws in the mirror; look instead for the miracles of your singular and unique existence.

JUNE 19
Ask for more

It is okay to ask for more than you have at this moment.
You are allowed to want, to desire, to expand the
space you occupy. The universe is not finite; it can hold
everything you want to be and more. You do not have to
shrink who you are or what you want in order to make
others more comfortable. Your desires are worthy of
recognition, support, and pursuit as long as they do not
harm or reduce the space that others seek to occupy as
well. The world is big enough for all our dreams.

JUNE 20
This will pass

You can make it through this moment, and the next.
Whatever moment you are in, it is temporary. The
passage of time can be difficult, but it can also be a gift,
moving us through and beyond moments that cause us
discomfort or difficulty. The constant flow of time can
soothe the deepest wounds and heal the most painful
scars. Just follow your breath from this moment to the
next and through the days. The flow of time carries away
both the good we'd like to hold on to and the difficult
moments that challenge us.

JUNE 21
Be spontaneous

You can invent the world, recreate it with your imagination. You can choose joy in any minute of the day, and you do not need the permission of anyone. Allow yourself to embrace possibility. Dance and sing whenever your heart calls you. Celebration can be found in any moment if you commit yourself to searching for it. You can make the choice, even if the results are not instantaneous. Look for the path toward joy, and set yourself on it. You can begin to walk it any minute you choose.

JUNE 22
Honor the light

One special day of the year the sun stays with us in the sky much longer than any other. On the longest day, the sun warms the earth and illuminates our skies, and night is short and mild. All over the planet in a thousand different ways, this day is celebrated for what it brings. It marks a point when the days begin to get shorter again, a natural ebb to the light that drives the seasons and corresponds to the spin of the earth. We begin to spin toward the cooler days and longer nights, a slow process that has repeated infinitely since long before we were born, so we can begin a shift of our own.

JUNE 23
Explore the depths

The ocean is deeper than you can imagine, filled with life as strange as science fiction. It is the great unexplored place here on our planet home. The mysteries of the ocean are as wild as the sea is wide. You contain just as much depth and as many mysteries. Your heart can weather the storms and waves of life, its beauty and depth undisturbed under the surface. What beautiful and strange things are waiting for you inside, impatient for you to explore?

JUNE 24
Imperfection is still meaningful

Everything you are in this minute is what you are meant to be, the sum of your choices and your experiences. When you worry that you are in some way flawed or broken, know that every imperfect piece of you makes you whole and perfectly unique. There is only one of you in the world, and so you cannot be broken. There is no one to compare you to, no ideal or perfect self you fail to measure up to. There is just you, as you are, doing the best you can. It is enough.

JUNE 25
Love is powerful

The world is full of powerful forces we cannot see, only feel. Love is no less real than the gravity that pulls us to the earth. The force of love shapes cultures and civilizations, builds families and communities that impact every facet of our lives. Love is beautifully renewable; it does not require material resources. It only requires your commitment to showing up, your commitment to forgiveness and embracing others. Love is radical, an invisible superpower you have in your hands right now.

JUNE 26
Nurture your curiosity

Your mind is capable of absorbing so much—every lesson from every mistake as well as every moment of joy. You are learning right now, in every moment. Knowledge doesn't just come from between the covers of books. Your interaction with others is a font of information and education. The natural world can teach you without ever needing to read a word. Let yourself learn in all directions, without limitation or fear.

JUNE 27
Invite in creativity

Creativity is not something you catch like a fish on the line. It comes when you cultivate a space for it, open up a door to invite in what it has to offer. In what ways are you able to make space for your own creativity? It will require that you pay attention to your curiosity and follow where it leads. Be open to being surprised by your own inspiration. Wander with it, and let it take you by the hand into new frontiers of imagination.

JUNE 28
Find your center

The world has you spinning like a top, constantly in motion as you try to tackle the challenges you face. Like a top, you have a center. Like a storm, in the middle there is an eye of potential calm. No matter what whirls around you, you can return to yourself and your breath. You can find your center—it is always there, waiting for you to step into a moment of peace. It does not solve any problem, it is not a resolution, but it is space to think and reflect, before you step out into the whirlwind once again.

JUNE 29
Illuminate the dark

If you cannot see the light, you do not need to stand still
in the darkness. Reach out a hand for the switch, for the
match, for the candle. You may trip and fall over unseen
obstacles, but you will find the illumination you search
for. To stand paralyzed without moving is to give up on all
possibility of light. The room may be absolutely filled with
candles, but without the match they will remain useless.
Without searching, how can you illuminate the dark?

JUNE 30
Transformation can go slowly

Every day, you change a little, shift a little, become a little
more yourself. We associate transformation with sudden
and dramatic change, but just as often, maybe more
often, transformation is a daily habit and a process of
change. It can happen so slowly that we are barely aware
of it, until one day we wake up and realize we are someone
new and unfamiliar. Get to know yourself as you are now,
and leave behind the assumptions you have about how or
who you should be. What will you discover?

July

JULY 1
Soak up the sunlight

There is no light like that of the sun, giving life to green things, illuminating all the corners of our world. Even on less than bright days, the warmth of the sun reminds us that there are things bigger than ourselves, and the world keeps turning. The whole world is growing and changing, thanks to this beautiful glow. Can you let it shine on your heart?

JULY 2
We depend on one another

We live together in a world that requires us to be connected and mutually dependent. Our sense of obligation to one another sometimes feels like a heavy burden, but it is also very precious. What we do for one another and what we do with one another, hand in hand, is what makes the world possible. What do you receive that you can give back to others? What can you receive to share with others? These exchanges are a beautiful expression of our interconnectedness and our collective love.

JULY 3
Imagination is limitless

There is no limit to your imagination. With your creativity, you can travel to places no one else has invented, meet people who have never existed. Travel backward in time, or forward; your imagination is a time machine, a spaceship, a magic wand. Use that power to invent new ways of being in your life, in your body. You can use it to solve problems you haven't even experienced yet. Whether you activate your imagination within the pages of a book or by staring at the clouds, you only need to give yourself permission to travel beyond.

JULY 4
A forest is a community

We think of a forest as something static, a backdrop
of the natural world, occupied by animals and plants,
an ecosystem. The forest is more than the sum of its
parts; it is a living organism made up of every life inside
it. Each tree and mushroom exists in a network of soil
like a nervous system; every bird is a transmitter. You're
not so different from a forest yourself. Filled with cells
and nerves, microorganisms and bacteria, you're a biome
too, a living community. The earth and you are alive in
the same ways, and you are as important a part of the
system of the earth as any mushroom or bird. How can
you connect with it?

JULY 5
You have permission to be flawed

Your capacity to love is not measured in moments or
mistakes. All of us can only do our best, and our hearts
are infinite in their ability to expand. Forgive yourself for
what you are unable to accomplish. Allow yourself the
grace to grow and do better in the future. As the days
unspool and you learn more, it is okay to become better.
Do not let your heart close to change and forgiveness.

JULY 6
Listen to your intuition

When was the last time that your gut told you something you could trust and act on? Each of us has our own finely tuned intuition, a combination of subconscious thought, guesswork, and just plain magic. It's a powerful tool that we can use to guide us through this world when we feel unsure or unsteady. If you tend to ignore or disregard the messages of your intuition, you may struggle to decipher its messages. But it is there for you however quietly it whispers, no matter how long you keep it waiting.

JULY 7
Be who you are

You don't need to be anything other than what you are right now, in this moment. Valid, strong, and resilient, your heart is perfect just as it is. Love is all around you, in as many shades as you can imagine. Allow it to feed you and expand your heart into new shapes and new territories. The journey of loving yourself will bring you places you cannot imagine, and joys you can only dream of.

JULY 8
The sun will return

Clouds and rain come and go. The sky cannot always be sunny, or we would not appreciate its warmth and power. With the changes of the sky come the different moods of the world, sometimes overcast, sometimes shining bright. The changes we experience help us understand the relationship between these cycles and appreciate the wonder of each part of the process: how rain gives life, how the clouds offer shade, and how the sun powers growth. Every cloudy day has its gifts, if you can look for them.

JULY 9
Change your mind

As we grow and learn, we cannot expect to stay the same as before. The process of change is the only constant in our lives. It can be difficult for the people in our lives to accept that we change as we grow, altering our beliefs and convictions, changing our minds. We can become entirely new people. But you do not owe anyone a static mind or a still, unchanging heart. The experiences of your life will change you, and that's okay.

JULY 10
Your heart is a garden

A garden grows in your heart, planted with the seeds
you sow and tended by your choices and actions. You
can choose to plant in rows, carefully cultivating specific
blooms, but hearts can be unruly things. Sometimes they
bloom with flowers that you did not expect, surprising
you with their strength, their vibrance, their beauty.
Sometimes weeds spring up that need your careful
intention and attention. Just like the gardens outside, a
heart is a beautiful and unpredictable thing. Make sure
you tend it well.

JULY 11
Rest is an active choice

You do not have to be constantly in motion. You can
pause whenever you need, whenever your body demands
it. Are you listening to what your body is asking you?
The world whirls around us constantly, calling for us to
participate. It is so difficult to slow down and give the
body what it needs. But every single one of us needs rest.
There is no one who can really give permission to do so
except yourself. You do not have to be perfect, or have
achieved every goal. You only need to stop, even for a few
moments, to breathe.

JULY 12
Transformation is happening now

What are you becoming? Even now, in this moment, you are changing! Can you feel it? You are not the same person from one moment to the next; you go through cycles of growth and rebirth just like the trees. Sometimes you bud and grow, sometimes you are as colorful as a sunset, sometimes you are shedding what is no longer useful. What an opportunity to reinvent yourself at every turn, to ebb and flow with the tides. To change is as natural as the turning of the seasons.

JULY 13
Clouds are only passing

When you cannot see the sun, do you begin to doubt that it can shine on you? The clouds can hide some of its light, but you can still feel it, see its impact. The clouds are only temporary, necessary bringers of shade and rain. Trust that good things are behind the clouds, and the clouds that come are necessary. The rain will pass, and flowers will bloom in its wake, under the sun.

JULY 14
Feel the earth

When was the last time you put your bare feet on the earth? We spend hours indoors, protected by shoes and rugs and floors. Underneath every street and road the earth is cradling you, holding you steady and firm. If you have the opportunity, shed the socks and shoes and floors, and step out into the world. Connect to it directly; allow yourself to come in contact unmediated and free. Touch the ground, and say hello to an old friend.

JULY 15
Strength can be delicate

A butterfly is a precious and delicate thing, a metaphor we use to signify fragility. But a butterfly also migrates across vast continents, flying farther than many people will go in their lifetime. Its paper-thin wings bring it north to south, visiting thousands of flower blooms along the way. In many respects, it is a signifier of resilience alongside its delicacy and beauty. A beautiful thing can be both strong and tender, gentle and powerful. And so can you.

JULY 16
It's okay to be alone

The company we keep shapes us and makes us who we are. So what is the impact of keeping company with ourselves? It's so important that we be comfortable and joyful in our company, alone with ourselves. Loneliness happens to all of us, but we can find ease and comfort in being alone. Our friendships can shape us, but ultimately who we are is a product of the choices we make inside our own heads when we keep our own counsel. Do you enjoy spending time with yourself? Can you cultivate that joy the way you would the company of a friend?

JULY 17
Honor your word

Have you given your word? The agreements we make to one another help us build a community and join our hands in friendship, partnership, and solidarity. It can be tricky to honor our own hearts and still keep our promises. It's a delicate balance of boundaries and obligations. How we navigate these negotiations is what determines our character. Commitment to one another is not supposed to be easy, though in moments it can be. Seeing it through and finding the spaces of joy are what give our relationships meaning.

JULY 18
Relationships are complicated

Our relationships are as subject to transformation as
we are. The bonds between one another are complex
and fraught with misunderstanding and confusion. We
hurt each other, accidentally or on purpose. We offer or
withhold forgiveness according to the pain in our heart.
But every relationship holds a seed of reconciliation. That
does not mean that things broken can always be repaired
in the same way. But a door can be opened to a new way
to be. All it requires is an open heart and a mutual hope
to heal.

JULY 19
Say farewell to the day

As the day fades and twilight blends starlight into the sky, the world begins to sleep. Before it does so, it sings you a lullaby. The birds, the insects, the humans winding down their day—it all calls to you. Open a window and let it in. The warmth of the night and the gentle breeze beckon you toward your dreams, toward rest. Let yourself be invited by its gentleness.

JULY 20
Trust the process

So many of the moments of our life are only intelligible through the rearview mirror. In hindsight, what felt like chaos in the moment becomes a path, a journey, a cohesive thread that ties our past to our future. Even now, we are spinning that thread, no matter how driven or aimless we feel. The path through our lives is only visible when we turn around to reflect on it. In the meantime, in the present, we grasp and twist, stretch and guess, trying to find the correct path forward. Trust that where you are now will make sense later. Trust that the thread will unwind in its own time and way, and that you will arrive to reflect on where you have been.

JULY 21
We are all one

In Buddhism, the nature of existence is described as fundamentally interconnected. Each of us can trace a path from ourselves to each other, from others to the world around us. We cannot exist without one another. The sun is as much a part of us as our skin, the ocean is as much as part of us as our tears. The world spins because you are here, and it could not be any other way. You are as important as the moon in the sky, and so is every stone and blade of grass in the field.

JULY 22
Savor the good memories

Your memories are a place only you can visit, a prism through which you view the story of your life. The mind has a talent for retaining the highs and lows, passing over the mediocre and the routine in favor of what leaves the most powerful impression. It's worth deeply considering what memories you hold dear, so they can function as a touchstone in your life. How do they shape who you are now? And how have they changed with you as time has passed?

JULY 23
Look for the beauty

Look at the world—really look. Can you count every leaf that sparkles and shines in the sunlight? The world is full of beauty in every direction, in every season and moment. In some seasons, it is harder to spot. Your eyes can be clouded, distracted by what is difficult or ugly. The world contains both in equal measure, and it is up to you to choose what to take into your heart. Do not look away from what is less than beautiful, but appreciate with all your heart what is.

JULY 24
The future is waiting

None of us knows what comes next. The future is an unexplored country, utterly unknown. We must face it together, hand in hand. It requires that each of us be brave, but you are equal to whatever challenges that will come. The future can be explored and named together if you are able to build your community and reach toward better things. You can shape the future with your love, your commitment, your passion, and your inspiration. It is waiting for you.

JULY 25
Get moving

Do not let yourself grow static and stiff. Movement is one of the great sources of joy. Your body can feel the rhythm of a song, the grace of a dance, the press of a hand in yours. Let yourself sway, wiggle, and bend. Do not think about what you look like—the only audience you need is yourself. Listen to how your body responds. Consider deeply what it needs, what movements feel good. Toss aside whatever does not resonate with your spirit. Move in whatever way feels right, but make sure you move!

JULY 26
Explore the world

If you were infinitely brave, where would you go? The truth is, you do not need an unending reservoir of courage to strike out on your adventure. Your heart is strong enough to face its fears, and move beyond them. The only way to explore everything the world has to offer is to harness your bravery, whatever there is of it. You will surprise yourself, find that the well you tap can fill and fill again. With exploration comes new information about yourself and what you are capable of. You will find you have plenty.

JULY 27
Beauty is waiting

Picture a field sown with every type of grass and flower you can imagine. Let it stretch to the horizon, an endless wildflower prairie in the gentle sun. Imagine what it would be like to lie with the grass at your back and all around you like a mattress of the freshest green. This field is just part of a whole landscape of beauty, waiting to embrace you. The world can do this too—find the people and places that make you feel held in beauty.

JULY 28
Cherish joy

They may be fleeting, but wonder and joy are fundamental to our lives, bringing us forward, illuminating what is worthwhile. Allow yourself to feel it! Embrace the expansiveness of your own joy, the good things in your life. It's important to recognize your joy and celebrate it, even if it cannot be pinned in place.

JULY 29
We are strong together

The smallest grains of sand can be picked up by the wind, blown across oceans, and carried around the world. Together, sand grains can become a desert, or hold back the tides and floodwaters. By itself, a grain of sand cannot hold back the water or the wind. It cannot stop a wave. En masse, the sand is a powerful force itself. Bound together into walls of concrete, it can reach toward the sky, building skyscrapers. What can you do when you are bound to others, sharing the same goals and bearing a shared weight?

JULY 30
Trust the timing

The universe keeps its plans to itself, operating on a clock that you cannot see, measured not in minutes but in moments that stretch long and short depending on our emotions. You cannot rush the universe; its plans will unfold on a scale that you can only see a small corner of. It's perfectly natural to want to plan for what you want, setting to work to achieve your goals. After all, the universe rarely hands you an opportunity you haven't prepared for in some way. Do your thing, and let the universe do its own, in its own time.

JULY 31
You are powerful

Even when you feel overwhelmed, there are options you have not yet explored. Your power exists in the many ways you can act on the world around you. You can reach out to others and join your power together, organizing action together for a better world. Even a single act by a lone person can change the course of the world; it can certainly change your life. How will you transform the world with your choices?

August

AUGUST 1
Confidence is a practice

Building in your heart is a combination of faith, comfort, and enthusiasm—your confidence. You are so capable and ready to take on the world, even if you feel unsure in this moment. Think of a moment when you were so sure you were in the right place at the right time. Can you conjure that moment again for yourself? Your confidence is inside you, just waiting for you to beckon it forward.

AUGUST 2
You are capable of more

There are many risks on the road to greatness.
You cannot step into your full potential without being
challenged, without trying and failing. To become greater
than you are, to step into your power, you have to move
forward. You have to push yourself, to want and reach
for more. There's no one way to sharpen your focus, to
embrace the challenges of life and overcome them, but
you can face them bravely. You are capable of greatness.

AUGUST 3
Dance for yourself

If you hear a tune, do you move to its music? When a beat moves through your bones, do you sway? Music is an invitation for your body to join in with the dance of life. Don't be afraid to experience the wild adventure of movement and expression. Dance is fundamental to who we are as people, and it helps us connect to our feelings and loosen the stiffness of both heart and body. Let yourself move!

AUGUST 4
Try again

Every time you try again, you can try something a
little differently. Every time you shift something in you,
you create a new chance at success. Refining your
approach, creating new versions of your paths and plans
with every new attempt: this is called iteration. Each time
this happens, you can learn more about yourself, about
the world around you, and about how it works. You can try
as many times as you like. You will always learn more.

AUGUST 5
Think of the bigger picture

Your day-to-day life contains an infinite amount of
choices and distractions. It's perfectly normal for you
to feel bogged down in the details, focused on the daily
expressions of concerns. The bigger picture is easy to
miss in the shuffle. When you feel overwhelmed by the
scale of your concerns and your worries, try to focus on
the larger narrative of your life, the people who love you,
and the things that make your world large.

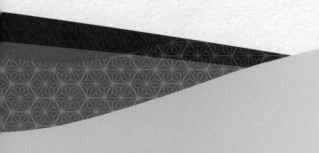

AUGUST 6
Your limits are a tool

You are capable of so much, but even you have your limitations. Don't let the limits of your abilities distress you. Every person has their own unique set of constraints they have to work within. You can push against them, stretch them, but ultimately you will have to accept the final edges of yourself. Constraint can birth creativity, give you structure to build on, and strengthen your resolve. Can you learn to work with it, rather than to fight it?

AUGUST 7
Offer respect

You will not get along with every person you meet, or agree with every decision the people around you make. There will always be differences, things that will separate and divide. Sometimes, the only common ground we can reach is a field of mutual respect. Respect is a kind of love that we are all entitled to, whether or not we can share affection or joy. We all deserve dignity, to live safely and peacefully. When you cannot extend any other kind of love, respect is always there to offer.

AUGUST 8
Your heart speaks to you

It is not always thrilling or joyful, but it is the truest voice that will speak to you. What is inside your heart cannot be contained. It speaks in a voice that only you will understand, only you can decipher. You are in charge of untangling the messages of your heart, and no one can read them—or act on them—but you. Where will you allow these missives to take you?

AUGUST 9
Find your calm

To create a sense of calm in a chaotic world is no easy task. You have to seize moments of ease and joy when they come, and craft a life in which moments of peace are welcomed when they arrive. How can you invite more calm into your life? Whether it's cultivating a meditation or breathing practice or using exercise to settle your heart, you have a measure of control over your sense of calm. Invite it into your day with intention.

AUGUST 10
Zoom in

When you feel that the world is much too large and complicated for you to grasp, let it fall away. Zoom in close. Choose something to focus on: a favorite plant, a candle, a book. Give yourself permission to engage deeply with a quiet and peaceful moment. It's okay to allow yourself a break from trying to solve every problem. It only has to be temporary. You do not have to release your obligations or your plans. Just let your brain release for a few moments.

AUGUST 11
Expand your view

Your heart can hold more than you can ever imagine.
A whole world is waiting to be welcomed into it. The wide,
wide borders of the space inside your heart can contain
everything you will ever learn and ever be, everyone you
will ever love (and all those you need to forgive as well).
It can contain every person you have been, and every
person you will be in addition to who you are now. Don't be
afraid to become larger, take up more space in your own
heart and the world.

AUGUST 12
Celebrate others

When you feel a twinge of envy, what is it that you really feel? Sort through the feelings—there is desire to have or to be something else, a fear that you cannot claim that for yourself. See this feeling as a guide to what you want, rather than a reason to feel negatively about others. Celebrate with them, and allow thoughtful reflection to be your guide as you process your feelings.

AUGUST 13
Hear the music

The frogs are croaking, the bugs are buzzing, the birds are singing. Even the wind has its own song as it moves through the trees and past your window. When was the last time you stopped to listen to the music of the world around you? Even a city sings in sirens and radios. We humans are so good at making music, but we struggle to hear the music all around us, the songs that do not need our participation. They are playing just for you. Will you stop to hear the concert?

AUGUST 14
Routine is restful

There is no shame in changing; neither is there shame in consistency. To wake up each day and live it like the last is a gift in and of itself. We prioritize novelty and excitement, but the rhythm of routine allows us to appreciate the small and important joys in our life: family, friends, a good cup of something warm in the morning. What do you return to that still gives you joy, however many times you experience it? Allow yourself to make space for what warms your heart no matter how much time passes or how familiar it might be.

AUGUST 15
Develop your ability to be intentional

Your intentions share every action. With firm and specific intention, even the most boring chore can become a ritual. The power of intention is that it dedicates our action toward a goal, making us more mindful and focused. Intentions can be as large as a New Year's resolution or as small as the choice to remain mindful as you walk down the street. To be more intentional is to cultivate a better awareness of why and how you do the things you do, and improve the quality of your life through that mindfulness.

AUGUST 16
Skip like a stone

Have you ever skipped a stone across the surface of the water, bouncing it lightly over a surface when it should sink? You too can move that way over the surface of the world, bouncing what should sink with a lightness of touch. Let your sense of purpose move you forward, keep you focused on your goal and direction. You can be serious and sturdy, but still fly straight and true.

AUGUST 17
You are more resilient than you realize

One of the most wonderful qualities that humans possess is our resilience. We are incredibly flexible, remarkably adaptive, and capable of change. You can change the course of your life, choose transformation or redemption at any point. But your resilience doesn't only shine in your darkest or biggest moments. Each day you wake up and greet a new morning full of opportunity. Your ability to welcome it with open arms despite past challenges is wonderful, too.

AUGUST 18
Nature has its own patterns

The tides are tricky; each day they rise and fall a little
differently. Watch them for only a few days and you will
struggle to work out their patterns. You will find yourself
focused on the waves that come and go, the endless
repetition. But the tides have their reasons, and their
own relationship. The waves are one cycle inside the
tides, the tides are a cycle inside the waxing and the
waning of the moon, patterns inside patterns. Only your
mindful attention, devoted and thoughtful, will unlock the
cycles and help bear you to your destination.

AUGUST 19
Watch the sun rise

Every day the sun rises, and you wake up to a new day.
The turn from dawn to light is easy to forget about as
you dive into your day. But the sun rises each day in a
blaze of color and joy, sliding up above the horizon. It
turns the clouds to flags and eclipses the stars, shining
bright to bring the dawn. Whether you choose to rise
with the sun or wake up to it already beaming into your
window, remember what a miracle it is that our star
warms us so gently and reliably.

AUGUST 20
Close your eyes

You have a secret superpower that you take for granted. You use it every minute or so without even thinking about it. What is this power? You can close your eyes and retreat to the sanctuary of your mind. While a blink is not a break, you can extend that blink into a break anytime. Rest your eyes, and process your thoughts. Claim a moment of stillness for yourself, wherever you are. Maybe it cannot change the world, but you'll be surprised what even a moment's pause can do for your outlook.

AUGUST 21
Be generous

There is so much space in the world to share, and to give. There is more than enough for all of us, for you and for everyone you love, but also for anyone you can imagine. Every empty hand could be filled. It starts with you and your own generosity. Give what you have with a generous hand, both your resources and your kindness, forgiveness, and grace. Give it to others whenever you can, and give to yourself as well. Generosity starts at home.

AUGUST 22
You can't please everyone

Each of us is fallible and flawed, prone to making mistakes. What's more, sometimes you simply cannot measure up to the high standards you set for yourself, or that others set for you. At some point, you will disappoint someone you love or admire. But disappointment cannot stop you from learning or from moving forward. In the best-case scenario, you can learn from disappointments. Disappointment happens; disappointment passes. Do not let it stop you from trying again.

AUGUST 23
Express your appreciation

When was the last time you told the people in your life how much you appreciate them? It is so easy to chase through the patterns of our days without being fully aware of how many people touch our lives and make them possible. The scale of it can crack your heart open in the best way possible. Today, make sure you express your appreciation when you bump into the gifts of other people. Open the way for them to express their appreciation of you as well. You touch many lives, and that is a gift, too.

AUGUST 24
Make promises and keep them

The promises we make to one another form the foundation of our collective lives. Even the small promises we make are important, bringing us closer to each other. Honoring those commitments, large and small, helps us keep the faith and chart a stable course into the future.

AUGUST 25
You stand on the shore

The waves come and go, sometimes gently kissing the shore, sometimes crashing down. Where they meet the land, the view is clear and far. Though they rise and fall, moving in tides, they are persistent in their mission, which is only to arrive. You have the same mission, only to arrive in each new moment, ready for a new shore.

AUGUST 26
Tell your story

The stories we tell about our lives shape us and make us who we are as people. Assigning roles and divvying out parts, scripting and revising and reimagining—it's all how we process what happens to us. The facts may be fixed, but the framework can shift as your worldview shifts, as how you see yourself changes and expands. Your life is full of adventure and love, rich enough for an epic poem or a novel. Do you see yourself as the hero of your own story?

AUGUST 27
Grow like a tree

A tree does not grow alone. As a sprout, it is protected by the other trees around it. As it matures, it collects energy, storing and sharing it. In time, it reaches high, delicately navigating shared airspace with its neighbors. Below, its roots stretch network to network, a fine weaving of interlaced communication. We think of ourselves as very different from trees, but we both occupy this world in so many of the same ways. Trees are not just backdrops; they live lives of their own and grow communities around them.

AUGUST 28
Learn

The world is waiting in every page and on every journey. There is room in your mind for so much more than you realize. It is as expansive as the sky and deeper than the ocean, capable of as much joy as the longest parade. Your mind has the capacity to travel beyond the farthest star and tallest mountain. Stretch your limbs as far as they will go and let your feet wander. You are capable of learning so much, so get going.

AUGUST 29
Move forward

Momentum keeps you changing, keeps you in motion. It allows you to see the world with fresh eyes each day, moving you forward. But it is easy to get swept up in the forward motion and lose track of where you are headed. Your destination may feel out of reach, however swiftly you might be moving. There's no need to charge ahead just for the sake of it. Don't be afraid to slow down and consider why—and where—you are rushing off to so quickly.

AUGUST 30
Watch for the signs

Are your eyes open to the signs the universe sends your way? The world around you speaks to you in many voices, in many ways and methods of wisdom. Your intuition can guide you and help you listen, help you look. If you are feeling lost, slow down and look for directions. Ask questions, and look for answers. Make space to reflect, and invite silence so you can listen closely to the messages of your own heart.

AUGUST 31
Keep the faith

Life has its ups and downs, and when things are difficult, it can be hard to remember that better moments are coming. Optimism is a kind of faith, positivity is a kind of faith—anything that reminds you that things will get better and asks you to believe in the potential of the future. All it asks of you is that you take the next step forward, even if you do not know exactly what is in store. There is so much waiting for you. What will you discover when your faith is rewarded by stepping into the future?

September

SEPTEMBER 1
Find your routine

Every day is new and different, but it is the rituals and routines of daily life that ground and sustain us. Our routines often get a bad rap, associated with stagnation and ruts, but they also help us build structure and give us momentum. They hone our impulses and intentions into habits that help us achieve our goals. What in your routine is supporting your intentions, and what is less helpful? Allow yourself to prune what is not working for you, and cultivate your routines with thoughtfulness, letting them grow.

SEPTEMBER 2
Stand in the trees

Long fingers reaching toward the sky, decorated with colorful flags or bare, breathing in and out—the trees all around you are a community of individuals as unique as you and your loved ones. You pass them every day, patient watchers recording history in their rings, standing through seasons. They take each moment as it comes, and teach lessons if we are willing to listen. Steadiness is its own virtue, and so is the ability to take the seasons of life as they come.

SEPTEMBER 3
Look for truth

What you believe to be true shifts like a prism, looking different from each angle. What is true is that the truth is always multifold, viewed through as many eyes and perspectives as you can imagine, tinted and colored by the experiences and reflections of others. At the center are the things that are true for everyone. Can you make space for the variety of experiences and perspectives while still holding fast to the hard realities of the world?

SEPTEMBER 4
Let the waves come

Everything comes in waves, arriving, crashing onto you, departing into the past. The waves on the surface of the sea can be gentle or overpowering in their fury and violence, but underneath the sea is quiet and constant, filled with life. Only the edges of the shore erode and change. The tides may pull in and out, shifting with the ebb and flow of the moon and the season, but these are passing moods. The cycles of the surface do not change the essence of the sea, nor its power.

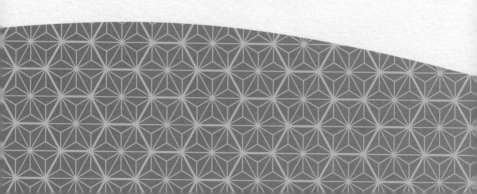

SEPTEMBER 5
Your destination will surprise you

Every moment is a step you take forward on the long and surprising road of your life. You don't have to know where you are headed exactly, but having a destination in mind helps you direct your forward motion toward a goal. You can change your destination whenever you want, and it may even shock you when you arrive. Consider your steps, tread lightly, allow for shifts and surprises. Shape the destination with every move.

SEPTEMBER 6
Respect your boundaries

The lines you draw around your heart can contain your joy or keep out what could harm you. How you hold those lines is entirely up to you; you can be firm and steadfast or flexible and porous. Your boundaries do not have to be walls or a fortress that you build for your heart. You can leave the doors and windows open if you choose. You can move the fences, dismantling whatever no longer brings you joy. What is most important is that you do so with intention, not out of habit or fear. Boundaries are a house you have to live in; make sure you feel good dwelling inside them.

SEPTEMBER 7
Imagine the future

The world is ripe with possibility if you allow yourself
to imagine it. The future is not just the site of your
anxieties and fears, but also the total sum of your plans,
hopes, and potential. Can you embrace both sides of the
coin? Change and growth are only possible if you move
forward into the future, a place to create the world and
yourself anew.

SEPTEMBER 8
Stay humble

Self-awareness is a balance of confidence and humility.
There's no need to feel imposter syndrome or doubt your
abilities. You can do so much, and you are so capable! But
the other side of a healthy sense of your own worth is
understanding what you do not know, what you have left
to learn, and what others can teach you. What you don't
know is a gift, an opportunity to grow and change. Make
space for it and your capacity to learn.

SEPTEMBER 9
Take the leap

There's a huge empty space in front of you called the future. It's an edge, a shore, a wilderness unexplored. Are you brave enough to jump into the wide expanse? One of the hardest things you will do is leap into this unknown, and if you are lucky, you will have the opportunity to do it frequently. If you do it often enough, you might even find you learn to fly.

SEPTEMBER 10
Invite luck in

We think of luck as something nebulous and fleeting, rather than something we can draw to us. But luck is something you can make, remaining open and flexible to opportunities that come your way. You can charm luck, tempt it, lure it into your open embrace. The world is a dance, and to join in is to cultivate luck as your dance partner. Invite opportunity in, and say yes to what it asks of you.

SEPTEMBER 11
Recognize burnout

Pushing yourself beyond your limits is a healthy exercise, and necessary for learning what you are capable of. Part of the process, however, is assessing when you need to push and when you need to pause. Pushing too hard will cause you to burn out, flattening your spirit and exhausting your body. When you feel that you are approaching burnout, pushing too hard for too long, learn how to rest and repair. Give yourself space to take a break. The work will be there waiting for you.

SEPTEMBER 12
Routine supports your growth

If we had to make a fresh choice every minute of the day, we'd exhaust our ability to make choices. By the time breakfast was over, we'd have made a thousand tiny carefully considered choices and we'd have worn out our brain on things that we don't need to focus on. Routine is the solution—the same habits each day, no consideration needed when you choose how to take your coffee, or what path to take to work. Routine is a gift that frees up space in your brain for bigger thoughts. Invest time and energy in routines that make you feel good, and you'll have more energy for bigger decisions.

SEPTEMBER 13
Recognize when you are satisfied

What do you need at this moment? For all of us, life is filled with desire and grasping. Being satisfied with who you are and what you have is one of the most difficult parts of being human. The mind and heart are constantly chasing after what comes next, or what has already happened. Cultivating gratitude for the present moment and what is already in your hands is the only surefire way to reduce the constant drum of want. All you need to get started is to begin reflecting on what good you have, right now.

SEPTEMBER 14
Dream big

What you hold close to your heart emerges when your body is at rest and your mind is free to wander. Sometimes what you find is absurd, but it's also the space in which your hopes and fears play out. Your subconscious is busy processing, considering, and resolving while you sleep. It's not a coincidence that we use the same word—dream—for these subconscious moments and our deepest desires, because they can confuse and surprise us in the same way. Open yourself to the messages in your nighttime adventures, and see what they can tell you about your hopes and desires.

SEPTEMBER 15
Find your anchor

Life can be profoundly overwhelming, a torrent of experience, information, and reactions constantly engulfing you. The flood of daily life can make you feel like you're drowning. Build yourself a raft. Whether you find solace in pursuing a hobby, reflecting in a journal, taking care of your body, or being in the company of others, ask yourself what slows the flow to a manageable level. Make it a point to find the things that bring you joy, that anchor you and make you feel secure, stable, and safe, no matter what inundates you.

SEPTEMBER 16
Transform the old

In the cool and damp, mushrooms are able to transform what's old, dead, and fading into beauty and energy. Building structure out of the smallest filaments, swelling with dynamic forms and colors, mushrooms can be as beautiful as flowers and as powerful as trees while they convert what has been discarded into something useful. Thus transformed, those materials rejoin the cycle of life, an incredibly useful service. Can you use the mushroom as a role model for reviving parts of yourself and the world that need compassionate attention?

SEPTEMBER 17
Listen for harmony

The universe has its own music, everything in rhythm. There's a dance to the cycles of life and the balance of its forces. Disparate elements combine for the most sublime effects. Your role is just part of the chorus, harmony and melody, played in concert with every other living (and nonliving) thing around you. When it feels like a wrong note sounds, trust that it is part of the composition. You may not see the conductor, but the music plays on.

SEPTEMBER 18
Embrace depth

The blue sky hangs above you; when was the last time you looked deeply at it? The sky is deeper than the ocean, the widest thing you can imagine. It's easy to think of it as simply blue, a simple fact of life with a simple color. But if you take time with it, the sky is more shades of blue than the dictionary can name, and is full of secrets. Your mind is as wide, your heart is as deep; spend time with these deep things all around you.

SEPTEMBER 19
Let the sun set

The sun rises and sets each day, and it's easy to forget how much beauty the repetition creates. But each morning it graces the sky with a blush of color, and closes the day with a flame. Make an appointment with the sun to recognize its departure. Not all of us enjoy rising with it in the morning, but all of us can watch it slip beneath the horizon, and thank it for the light it sheds on our day.

SEPTEMBER 20
You cannot be everything

Life is full of potential, but even life has constraints. You cannot be everything to everyone. There will be paths that close when you make a choice, selves you must say goodbye to in order to become someone new. Potential must be selected and crafted into decisions and actions; otherwise, it goes unrealized. Give yourself permission to make those choices, and permission to reflect on what you did not choose, but do not stop becoming who you are meant to be.

SEPTEMBER 21
Flow

When you move in the smallest motion, you send ripples through your life. Stirring your tea, blinking your eyes, washing your hands—it's all important. Can you feel the universe moving through you? If you cannot, your breath is waiting for you to tap into the flow. Breathe in, and breathe out. The flow of your breath is flowing through you, through the universe, connecting you with everything and everyone. Let it flow. Listen, and let it guide you.

SEPTEMBER 22
Befriend your ambition

What secret desires do you keep in your innermost heart? Why keep them locked inside instead of bringing them into the light? It's okay to want more for yourself, to grow beyond the confines of expectation and become something new. To achieve your ambitions and dreams, you have to work hard for them and prioritize them. To give them that attention, you first have to acknowledge them. Give your desires space to breathe, and shed your shyness about what you want.

SEPTEMBER 23
Find perspective

From where you are standing, from the space you occupy, you can only see out from your own eyes. Of course, from where you stand, you look out from the center of your own universe. But you are not the center; every other person around you looks out from the center of their own personal and private universe, too. It's a powerful act of imagination to attempt to shift your perspective into the eyes of another, or into the eyes of many. Challenge yourself to do it as often as possible, and expand the view from where you are.

SEPTEMBER 24
Release control

Can you let go of your need to control the outcome
of the moment? You've done enough, unspooled your
effort through the days. It is impossible to predict
how the consequences of your actions will push through
the future of your own story and the stories of others.
Releasing your attachment to the results of your efforts
is difficult; releasing what was never in your control to
begin with is even more so.

SEPTEMBER 25
Energy is everywhere

We move through the world burning and consuming,
devouring energy and resources, but we also create
energy, pushing it out through every moment and out of
every pore. The world we live in is a constant exchange of
energy. The trees do it, the birds do it, the mushrooms
and worms under our feet are doing it, too. The cycle
is unending. Nothing is truly destroyed; everything is
created and recreated. How can you participate in the
cycle more intentionally, and more reflectively, to draw
strength and inspiration from this connection?

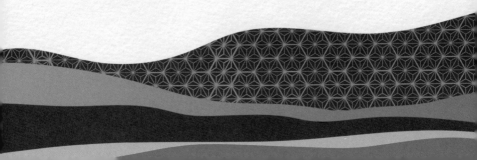

SEPTEMBER 26
Begin again

Every single moment is a new beginning. Every moment that passes is an ending. You can start anywhere, beginning the work you are waiting to do. You do not need a specific date or time; you do not need permission. Every single day is a new chance, a year can start anytime you choose. Don't wait! Start now. Make your own calendar, your own milestones, on your own time.

SEPTEMBER 27
Accept the past

Some things cannot be changed, such as immovable objects and facts of psychics. We cannot rewrite our histories, nor change the actions of others. In some moments, all we can do is move forward and give ourselves grace, and give grace to one another. What has happened cannot be undone, but we can always make new choices in the light of a new day.

SEPTEMBER 28
Shed your embarrassment

Have you done something that embarrasses you? It happens to everyone, but it doesn't lessen the sting of the moment. Things we have done long in the past can sneak back up on us, surprise us, knock us off balance long after they occur. You are better than your mistakes and mishaps, more than the sum of any one strange or difficult moment handled gracelessly. Forgive yourself, and release it.

SEPTEMBER 29
Make a new start

You can try as many times as you want. The results are not finite or fixed. You may not get the exact result you hope for, but there is always value in the attempt. Let your failures teach you about your skills, your limits, your desire, and your strengths. Your past attempts can and should inform the future. Nothing is wasted; keep going.

SEPTEMBER 30
Let yourself be surprised

You cannot predict every consequence, every twist and turn of your story. How wonderful—imagine if you knew everything that was coming! A life lived in exact expectation and wish fulfillment is an entirely boring one. The element of surprise creates excitement, allows you to experience things that you never could have dreamed of for yourself. Sometimes there will be things that disappoint you, cause you grief and sadness, or create difficulty. With them, you also receive joys beyond your imagination.

October

OCTOBER 1
Change will come

It's not always easy to change. Sometimes it feels like a perfect fit; other times, you have to shed your old ways like a snake shedding its skin, leaving you itchy and vulnerable. How do you know when change is right if it can be uncomfortable? Change opens doors into the future, allowing you to slither into something beautiful and new. Let yourself shed the things that you no longer need, and enjoy the feeling of the world on your new skin.

OCTOBER 2
Connect to the divine

Whatever you believe about the universe, it is filled with forces larger and more powerful than you. It's part of being in the world; none of us is larger than the whole. Honor the expansive power of the universe and the unending flow of time and consequences, whatever you call it. Some people connect with this relationship through organized religion or divinity; some explore it through the natural world. Whether you call this enormity by name or speak to it intimately, invite it into your heart, and take comfort in the fact that you are part of something bigger than yourself.

OCTOBER 3
Watch the leaves dance as they fall

When the daylight ebbs and the season turns cool with shorter days, the trees know long before you do. Even when you do not see it, they are slowly telling the leaves to rest, pulling their energy to be stored. The leaves that turn and fall have done so much—powered branches and roots, added a ring to the trunk to count the days. When they fall like fluttered flags, they are waving goodbye. Soon they will become something new, feed the soil, nourish the roots, joining new leaves in the future, creating sweetness once again.

OCTOBER 4
Express your admiration

The achievements of others are often spoken of in the context of envy, of desire, or of ambition. There are other ways to interact with the joy and success of others, other ways to fill your cup and fuel your inspiration. Celebrate the success of others! When you experience desire triggered by others, take it as a signal to guide your next step, not a challenge to what you have already. Let the recognition be a celebration, and share in the joy of success.

OCTOBER 5
Circumstances change

Wherever you are, you'll be moving soon. Circumstances change all the time as you receive new information and other people's choices move the pieces of your life into new arrangements. It is difficult sometimes to understand and cope with the shifts into new circumstances, even if they are positive. The universe is a vast and unexpected place, and its surprises can rock your foundation. Try to remember that whatever your circumstances are, they are temporary. Focus on what is in your control, and leave the rest up to the mystery of how the universe unfolds.

OCTOBER 6
Discomfort will pass

All things pass, both good and bad. Every moment of discomfort has its end, every moment of joy fades into memory. It can be a comfort to know that what is difficult will eventually be behind you, but that is so hard to remember in the moment. It does get better, and you are wonderfully resilient, capable of so much joy and love. You can move through this moment, and every moment, knowing something new awaits in the next.

OCTOBER 7
Let the fruit ripen

What starts as a bud transforms into a flower to call the bee. With pollination and time, the bloom transforms into a vessel, full of seeds and sweetness. What was beautiful in the spring became hard, softening only with time and patience to a new way of expressing color, form, and tantalizing temptation. All an unripe fruit requires from you is your time. As it ripens on the tree, it is busy doing its own work. When the time is right, reach out your hand for what it shares with you.

OCTOBER 8
Build your nest

When the weather turns cool and the days are shortening, we turn our attention to the interior, just like any other animal preparing for winter. How can you bring the natural world inside with you, staying connected even in retreat? Feather your nest with things that will remind you of the cycle of growth. The green will return in its own good time, after both you and the natural world receive your well-earned rest.

OCTOBER 9
Nurture tenderness

Tenderness is a gift that you can nurture in yourself, passing along this support to others. The world can hold your strength and your gentleness, and it needs both. Let your heart stay soft, flexible, and open. The world may make this challenging, but it's necessary and important to remain available to the sweetness it still contains. If you can keep a hold on your own capacity for softness, you can give it back to the world tenfold, and make it easier for others to be tender, too.

OCTOBER 10
Preparation is a practice

When the cycle of the seasons bends toward harvesting long-laid plans and appreciating their abundant results, our minds turn as well toward new plans. What preparations can you make space for as you connect with your gratitude? The closing of one cycle is the beginning of another. Every conclusion is followed by another chapter, full of empty pages and new goals. Hold your arms open, and embrace both the results of past plans and the new potential together.

OCTOBER 11
Take it as it comes

So much of what happens in life is not within your control. You can fight the unfolding, or you can allow it to flow around you—that is what is in your control. Focus on what lies in your own two hands, and make the best out of what you can do and what you can hold. It's something you must undertake as a practice, easier said than done, but always available to help you move forward with grace and strength.

OCTOBER 12
Kindness is a strength

The world can be a difficult place in which to cultivate kindness. It wears us down and makes us desperate for solace, pushing us onto paths that give us less joy and grace. To create and extend kindness even in moments where it is not easy is a tricky proposition. You are capable of so much kindness, both toward yourself and toward others. You can make the choice in every moment to bring your kindness to it.

OCTOBER 13
Variety is the spice of life

Consistency is valuable, predictability is useful, but variation is what gives us joy and excitement. Novelty fuels us and inspires us, challenges us and creates growth. Allow yourself to treat every day as ripe with the potential for discovery. Try everything, even things that you are unsure of. Try things you are convinced you will not like or are not for you! You cannot predict what will bring you joy and help expand your horizons, so chart a course through places and experiences that are totally new.

OCTOBER 14
Care for others

We cannot move through the world alone. While love and vulnerability with others always has the potential for disappointment, it's vital to our hearts, and such a source of strength and joy. Don't shut your heart away just to protect it. The best way to preserve your tenderness and kindness is to use them constantly, and care for others as often as you can manage. Rather than spending down the balance of your love, caring for others will fill you and expand your ability to receive and hold care.

OCTOBER 15
Find your path

Your path through life will not be a straight line. It may not even be a single line at all. If you feel you have reached a dead end, jump! Leap in any direction, and find a new path at your feet where you land. Many of us double back, forging new paths a thousand times in our lives. Just because you have been walking in one direction does not mean your destination is a forgone conclusion. Spin, pivot, and dance your way backward if it brings you joy and fulfillment. A person can move in all directions, even circles, even waves, even abstract wiggles—all you need to move toward is what makes you feel whole.

OCTOBER 16
You are enough

You do not need to be more than you are, or go faster toward your destination. You will learn, and you will grow, and you will be better than you are now. Right now, just as you are, you are still enough. You do not need to pursue perfection to be enough, to be worthy. You can make mistakes, you can be vulnerable, you can be delicate or too much, and you will still be enough.

OCTOBER 17
We depend on one another

We rely on one another for so much; the world we live in is an intricate social network of dependence and interconnection. There is nothing in this world that we accomplish truly alone. We travel on roads built by other people's hands, feed ourselves with food that others have gathered and processed, fill our souls with art that other people have created. The only way to repay this interconnectedness is to help others and contribute in your own way.

OCTOBER 18
Seek justice

The universe hangs in a fine balance; nothing is perfect, but everything has its own logic and reason. You as a person have a role in this universe, to make it beautiful and more perfect. You can change the world, even as a small creature in a big universe. Chase a higher standard. You can help create a better, kinder, more just world with your own two hands. All you have to do is try.

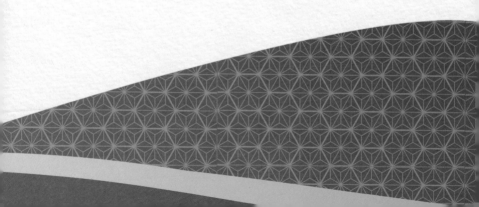

OCTOBER 19
Take care

You owe a debt of care to your body. You are not just a body moving through space, carrying around a brain inside a vessel. Your body, spirit, and heart are one unit, a holistic and interconnected set of selves that all require their own different kinds of care. When you feel tender, make sure you are giving your body what it needs: water, food, rest. The things that heal your body will also support your mind and your soul.

OCTOBER 20
Ask for help

There is no time in the world when you cannot ask for help. Help is not always obvious, it is not always accessible, and it is not always easy. Even with more hands, you will not erase the challenges you are facing. But what you can do is find solace and solidarity with others, share your experiences, and learn from the experiences of others. We can find solutions together; imperfect solutions together are better than challenges faced alone.

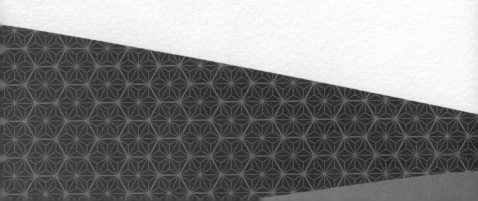

OCTOBER 21
It's okay to have regrets

Not one of us lives a life perfectly; to be human is to misstep, and learn from it. To regret without learning a lesson is just us feeding our anxieties, living in our past without relief. Do not be ashamed of the things you regret; if you listen to the lessons of things passed, there is no need. It's okay to let them shape you, inform your path through the world. But set yourself free from the weight of regret. Forgive yourself, and move forward.

OCTOBER 22
You are as strong as stone

Take inspiration from the earth. Solid and layered, durable and beautiful, even when stones shake loose and scatter, the earth is no less beautiful or complete. You may find that your challenges and experiences shake parts of you loose, transform the shape and feel of your heart. You are no less you for the changes, and no less resilient for being shaped by the impact of your experiences. Your strength and endurance allow you to survive, thrive, inviting in life at every turn. Under every tree and blade of glass, under the soil, stone provides a solid foundation.

OCTOBER 23
Mend what's broken

A break or tear is not a permanent ending. Most things can be mended, and sometimes the mending can create something more beautiful than what came before. In some Eastern cultures, a break in a delicate ceramic object is repaired with a precious metal like gold. The fix adds to the history, lends depth and strength, without trying to hide the damage. The mending and the solution are part of the beauty.

OCTOBER 24
Things happen for a reason

You will not be the same person you were yesterday today. What has happened occurred so you could be someone different in this moment, even when it is a difficult moment to bear. Every joy, every sorrow, every moment of learning has led you here, and will lead you farther than you can imagine. You do not need to know where you are headed, but you can trust that each moment will be a new adventure.

OCTOBER 25
Believe in miracles

Do you believe that miracles exist? You yourself are a miracle, one of a million possibilities. Each of us is a miracle in our own way; every moment we draw breath and live together is an incredible gift. In all the vastness of the universe, here we are together in this moment. The connection between each of us is wildly unlikely, insanely improbable. How lucky we are to be together here, on this planet, at this moment.

OCTOBER 26
Breathe in autumn

Can you smell the changing of the season? As the
summer unfurls and blooms, shifting into the abundant
harvest of autumn, it adds its own quality to the air.
The languor and ease of summer are replaced with a
snap and a breeze, a cool clarity and a light scent of decay.
The world shifts with it, allowing itself to consider a new
form of preparation and rest. How will you shift with
the season? Let your priorities change, and move with the
season into a new mental space.

OCTOBER 27
Look for your guides

Sometimes your purpose finds you, appearing with someone or something, guiding you forward. But more often you must find your purpose, working at it day by day, seeking it through trial and error. And when it does appear, it doesn't always lead you in a straightforward line. It may even change or shift as you do. Searching for your purpose will lead you to many places, but it will never lead you astray, only to new journeys and growth.

OCTOBER 28
Light your candle

What you have inside you casts its own unique light, the glow of your spirit illuminating the darkness of the world. The light is warm and generous, spilling outward for others to see. What sets you ablaze with joy? You can light others' flames as well, lighting a whole sea of candles against the dark to shine and inspire. As the days grow shorter, focus on how you can fill your days and nights with light even when you cannot see your own shine.

OCTOBER 29
Have faith

You cannot see the fullness of your path stretched out ahead of you. Every step you take forward is an act of faith in the future, that you are heading in the direction you were meant to go. Faith does not require a particular dogma or doctrine, though such things often demand faith. Faith is entwined with hope, and conviction, and humility; some things are unknowable but still important to the way we live our lives.

OCTOBER 30
The moon is waiting

The moon waxes and wanes, ebbs and flows.
Powerful enough to move the tides and gentle
enough to cool the nights, it is constantly changing.
Take your cues from the moon, and allow yourself
to ebb and flow as well. Don't be afraid of change,
or of seasons of darkness and light. Step into your
own light; move the tides of your life. Shift with the
needs of the hour or day. Appreciate the moments of
both fullness and darkness.

OCTOBER 31
Make magic

You can create magic with just your own two hands. You
are powerful beyond measure, full of intention and
potential. Can you feel the magic crackling inside you?
You can manifest the things you desire, with commitment,
work, and specificity. Your willpower is magic, a tool you
wield like a wand. Your heart is magic, an altar to what you
love and what inspires you. Don't hold back—cast your spell
on the world!

November

NOVEMBER 1
Honor your ancestors

You are the sum of a million, billion wishes, a sparkle and a dream in your ancestors' eyes. There are so many lives that have been poured into yours, so many dreams that have been chased to make your own dreams possible. What you do in the world is in no small part the sum of that whole journey. Do you consider this legacy in your plans? Think of it as a well of inspiration as much as it holds the weight of history. Investigate who came before you, find the through lines between you and those who came before you, and honor them when you can.

NOVEMBER 2
Share

What you have is not just yours. What you have, even after all your hard work and your dedication, is still the product of so many people. The people who have supported you, the network of resources around you, every teacher that led you forward: they gave you precious gifts, gifts that not everyone is lucky enough to receive. That leaves you in a position of power in which you can give that same gift to others. How can you offer support, give resources, lead others forward?

NOVEMBER 3
Lay down your burden

Do you feel heavy? It's likely you are carrying the weight of the world on your shoulders. Unclench your jaw and allow it to wiggle around. Roll your shoulders, sliding them down your back. Bring them down from your ears, expelling that tension from your body. Shake it out if it feels right. Release that weight, whatever you are carrying—you cannot carry the world alone every moment. It's not meant for you alone; it's meant to be shared. Set down the burden of responsibility and don't be afraid to ask for help.

NOVEMBER 4
Appreciate what you have

Your life is so very full: of love, of joy, of passion, of inspiration. Even in the quietest and most difficult moments, this is still true. When you cannot remember this, reach out your hands. Ask others who love you to remind you of what you have and how much you deserve the care and love they offer. What you have is beautiful, and what you have to offer others is equally so. Keep a list if you need it, and add to it daily. What blessings follow you and keep you afloat?

NOVEMBER 5
Wander

You can go wherever your heart leads you. You do not need a map—there is no map for a life unlived. No one can tell you which path to take that will bring you the most joy or avoid tremendous heartache. Every path you take will contain some measure of both, and the key is to take the steps that feel authentic and meaningful for you. Those are your true north, and your heart is the compass. Follow where it points, and throw away your maps.

NOVEMBER 6
Heal

There are times in life when your body is in need of more care than usual, when your body needs to fight and the only thing you can focus on is care. When you enter these moments, keep your perspective and weigh your priorities. Your health is deeply important; your body carries so much. It's not just carrying your beautiful heart and unique mind, but also the weight of expectations and desires, your hopes and your limits. When your body needs to come to the front of your attention, let it be the center of your concern.

NOVEMBER 7
Community is a form of care

What do you owe the people in your life? What we owe one another is part of our contract as a community—care, joy, love, respect, and accountability. Thinking about these obligations to one another can feel heavy, but it's an important responsibility and can be a powerful motivator to work toward growth and collective joy. Community is the foundation of our collective power to change the world for the better. Do not fear what binds you to others; let it be an outstretched hand rather than a burden.

NOVEMBER 8
You cannot please everyone

You are wonderful, but no matter how wonderful you are, not everyone will find you so. There will be many wonderful people in the world whom you do not like. There will be people who do not like you. If the feeling is mutual, there's no problem, only an agreement to part ways. You need not concern yourself with the people who do not like you; you cannot force them to, nor is it worthwhile to contort yourself into a new shape to be other than you are. Focus on learning self-awareness to distinguish between valid critique and sheer dislike, and save your energy for those who love you.

NOVEMBER 9
Take one day at a time

Today is only a matter of hours. You cannot leap forward through to the future; you cannot dive back into the past. You can only take things one day at a time, hour by hour, breath by breath. The days will move through their hours, the seasons through their cycles. There are days of cold and days filled with sunlight. Tomorrow, you will wake up in a new day, with a fresh start. There are no shortcuts, but it will arrive in its own good time.

NOVEMBER 10
Be brave

Are you ready? It's time to step forward into the unknown. The future is full of challenges, and you are more than equal to them. Those challenges will demand you to be bold, creative, and resilient. That does not mean that you need to be perfect, or that you cannot be afraid. We are all afraid, all confused, all imperfect. Bravery is not the absence of fear but the determination to overcome that fear and act anyway. You do not have to know the answer to try, but try anyway.

NOVEMBER 11
Let yourself grieve

Our hearts can crack open so easily. They are fragile, and so full of love. The departure of people we love, the unraveling of plans we've made, the mistake we make . . . all of these things can cause grief. It's okay for things to end; it's okay to make mistakes. Hearts break because they are tender and vulnerable things. But hearts also heal with time and care. They are strong, carrying you through everything you experience in your life. Don't be afraid for your heart; set it free to love and dream as much as you can bear. Your life will be richer for it.

NOVEMBER 12
You are the company you keep

The road of your life is filled with obstacles, twists, and turns. Everybody has their own road, but sometimes you will find company on the road where it meets with others. If you are lucky, they will be able to keep you company, traveling on parallel paths through the world. You might even learn from them, or take another path because of their guidance. These companions you keep will lighten your load, make it easier to travel. You can do it alone, but keep your eye out for those who can share in the journey.

NOVEMBER 13
Find gratitude

Every single moment is a gift, no matter how small or quiet. If you can live in that moment, you cultivate a sense of thankfulness. Every person in your life is a gift as well, and your gratitude for them is a gift in return. The more thanks you are able to give, the wider your heart becomes, a vessel for ever-increasing gratitude. What are you thankful for at this moment?

NOVEMBER 14
Get out of the grind

Are you tired? Set down your burden for a little while. You are so busy, so concerned with getting through the day and your tasks. You do not need to grind out every minute of the day to deserve your rest. You already deserve rest. Everyone deserves moments of peace, calm, and care. How will you carve out space and time for yourself? Honor the needs of your body.

NOVEMBER 15
Claim your self-sufficiency

While every one of us needs other people to help sustain our lives and build community, self-sufficiency is an important skill for both self-confidence and to be a good community member. You can do it; you are strong and resilient. What you can do for yourself can free up time and resources for others. Beyond that, the more than you can do for yourself, the more capable you will believe yourself to be.

NOVEMBER 16
Remember

Memory is magic, bringing the warmth of a pleasant day to a hard one, and sometimes felling a good moment with a stab of regret. Your memory shapes you, makes you who you are. As your memories blend and soften, they give an equal measure of joy and discomfort. Hold tight to the binding threads of memory that tie you to yourself, and make new memories that keep you moving forward.

NOVEMBER 17
Even trees rest

With their long and delicate fingers reaching toward the sky, trees are full of graceful beauty even in the dormant season. Swaying in the crisp wind, the empty branches of autumn trees frame the sky, soaking in the rain. They are waiting for the right time to burst into bloom, still alive and flexible in the cold. Just like the trees, you will have dormant seasons where you rest and wait. Your time will come again to bloom and stretch, but you can use the quiet to plan and recuperate, collect your thoughts and set your buds to wait for the sun.

NOVEMBER 18
Everyone is different

It's okay if you don't feel like anyone else. Each of us comes from an utterly unique lineage and set of experiences. While there's so much common ground to be found with others, no one will have lived a life exactly like yours. Your total uniqueness is beautiful, but it can also feel lonely to know you will never be perfectly seen or understood. Spend time understanding yourself to feel less alone. Journaling, therapy, even conversations with friends and loved ones can help you explicate who you are and help you feel less alone.

NOVEMBER 19
Cherish your family

The bonds we create sustain us, whether we are born to them or choose them. The people who are willing to be by our side through good and bad, celebrations and mistakes, joy and sadness—these are the people who deserve our whole heart. Give this circle of love your grace, your forgiveness, your excitement, and your difficulties, and let them surprise you with their capacity for love. Surprise yourself with your own ability to return that love, too.

NOVEMBER 20
Allow yourself to be taken care of

There's so much tenderness and sweetness in taking care of others, but you deserve to receive care, too. Do you allow yourself to receive care from others? Do you know how to ask for it when you need it? Offer yourself the gentleness you wish others could offer you. Take care and give yourself the space and time to feel valued, important, and loved. Figure out what makes you feel taken care of, and let others know what you need. No one is a mind reader, but your life is full of people who love you and want this for you.

NOVEMBER 21
Travel big and travel small

No matter how close you stay to home, you have the ability to step out and explore the world. Spread your wings and learn about yourself as well as others by broadening your horizons. If you can, let your feet wander far from your usual haunts, and see a different way of living in the world. When crossing physical distance isn't possible, travel with your eyes and mind—the library, the bookstore, and the internet are all full of ways of learning about the world, taking your imagination to other countries and even other realities. Let your soul wander widely, and you will learn so much.

NOVEMBER 22
Twilight is coming

The fading light has its own beauty, purple and blue, tinted with gold. The fading of the day is a place between, a hovering liminal set of moments washed with color, thick with transition. Your life has its own moments of twilight, the closing of one kind of being and the start of another. It can be complicated to see the beauty in the transition, but it is there working for you and waiting for you.

NOVEMBER 23
Love others authentically

Loving other people is not always easy, but it is deeply necessary. The most worthwhile things in life are often hard, and love is no exception. Everyone is flawed, everyone makes mistakes, and we often stumble into hurting or disappointing one another. It's important to maintain healthy boundaries and a high standard for how others treat us, but if someone fails you, discern whether they are genuinely seeking forgiveness and working to do better. If we make loving one another conditional on utter perfection in our relationships, life will be very lonely indeed. It's a standard no one can measure up to, including you.

NOVEMBER 24
Find your power

What feels unbearable has been borne before by others, and it can be borne by you as well. You are stronger than you realize, and more powerful than you can imagine. Your resilience will surprise you at every turn, and bring you new gifts each time you pass through something you thought you could not move beyond. Trust that you are capable, equal to this moment and every moment, even in moments where you cannot feel it.

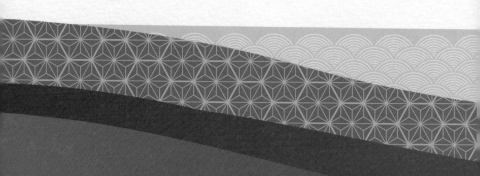

NOVEMBER 25
You have permission to fail

The only imperative in life is that you try your hardest. Success is not guaranteed, and you cannot predicate your self-worth on total success all the time. You can and will fail sometimes. You are allowed to fail! You are allowed to make mistakes, and try again. Change your approach, change your direction; you can even step away, let things go, say no to what no longer makes sense to you. Keep trying, keep learning, and don't be afraid to fail.

NOVEMBER 26
Feel all the emotions

Your emotions are a miracle, a potent cocktail of brain chemicals, physical responses, and spiritual resonances that shape how you see the world and the choices you make. The amazing range of what you feel can be overwhelming, and your emotions are a powerful force that aren't always in control. Learning to accept, process, and appreciate your emotions without letting them control every reaction is an important skill to help bring more intention into your life. You experience your emotions, but they don't have to be the boss of you!

NOVEMBER 27
Connection fuels your heart

What a balm for the soul other people can be! A conversation or even just a wave hello from a stranger you pass can bring joy and inspiration to a quiet day. We spend so much time seeking peace, quiet, and stillness as a remedy for our busy lives, but fellowship and friendship are also important to soothe the soul. When was the last time you called a friend just to say hello? Or got excited about a shared interest with someone new? Invite in joy through interaction and connection; the world is full of people who want to get excited and inspired with you.

NOVEMBER 28
You are blessed

Your blessings in this life are tangible; they have weight
and heft. If you tried to count them in full appreciation of
what you have, you would spend each moment in a litany
of remuneration. Even in moments where you cannot see
them, every cloud and raindrop is a blessing for you. Each
hand that grasps yours, each flower that blooms in your
eyes, is a moment of joy that feeds your soul.

NOVEMBER 29
Explore the unknown

What is out there in the wide world, waiting for you? The unknown is a mix of wonder and terror, and you are equal to it. You enter it one day at a time, keeping pace with the moment. It's full of surprises and excitement. Joy is also waiting out there for you to chase it. Every day has the potential to catch you off guard and change your direction. Take a chance and embrace what is waiting for you.

NOVEMBER 30
Your choices shape you

The choices you make also make you and shape the path you take through the world. Whether they are small or large, your choices in every moment have both intentional and unexpected consequences. Where they lead you will determine your future choices, and impact how other people see you. All you can do is be as thoughtful as possible when you make your decisions. Use all the available information, and trust your intuition to make the best possible choices you can.

December

DECEMBER 1
Every snowflake is unique

A snowflake is a small miracle, a perfect crystal formation falling from the sky to grace the landscape and kiss the ground. Small and delicate, it is nevertheless powerful, able to join with others to coat the world in insulated softness. Alone, it floats; together, snowflakes have a weight and heft that cannot be denied, shaping mountains and interrupting schedules. They do not need to be the same to join together and be powerful. Each of us is equally unique, and a total force of nature when we join together.

DECEMBER 2
Give

You have so much to give to the world, so much you can contribute to others. Each day you have a choice to give of yourself to the people around you. Small acts of care, even just sending a text, can reverberate through the recipient's life, allowing them to pass along the joy and kindness you extend to them. Giving is not just gifts and acts of charity. Your service, your kindness, and your work lighten someone else's load and make the world a better place, no gifts needed.

DECEMBER 3
Be alone with yourself

Being alone with ourselves can be difficult. The company of our own minds is not often the gentlest companion. Learning to be easy in our own company is a journey that we all embark on. The world is full of distractions, pulling us from ourselves with screens and sounds. The difference between being alone and loneliness is a fine, thin line that we can draw around ourselves. You do not need to be lonely in your own company; your heart is warm, and happy to be by your side.

DECEMBER 4
Warmth can come from within

Sometimes all we need is to feel tucked in, safe, and warm. We need to give ourselves the enveloping feeling of being valued and taken care of. Only you can give this to yourself, a cozier feeling than any blanket or cup of tea. Do you feel secure in the world, in your place in it? If not, ask yourself how you can create that feeling of coziness for yourself. It's not just about your physical surroundings, but also how you make a home for yourself and your heart in the world.

DECEMBER 5
Engage your senses

Crisp, clean, and chilly, the atmosphere of autumn is noticeable and distinct when the world exits fall and snuggles into the coldest season. It's the scent of evergreens and the wind on clean ice. It's the aroma of winter spices, rich and warming. The perfume of crackling wood in the fireplace, or dusty snow across an empty, patient field. Wherever you are and whatever your winter season brings, appreciate it for its own joys. It may not have the blooming scent of flowers or the richness of a humid day, but it has delights all its own, and its own part in the cycle of the seasons.

DECEMBER 6
Look for the bright spot

The world is quiet in the winter, with so many plants and animals in dormancy and hibernation. It's common to dismiss it as flat and colorless, but look closely. The rich green of the evergreen boughs, the pop of red berries that decorate it, the blaze of color in the sunrise and sunset behind bare trees—these are best appreciated now, where they are the star of the show. They fade to the background in busier seasons, but in winter they have their own radiant beauty.

DECEMBER 7
Let yourself believe

Your convictions, your faith, your beliefs—these things make you who you are. It's okay if they shift and change as you grow. It's only natural that as you learn more, what you believe about yourself and the world expands. Allow yourself the grace to grow. Forgive yourself if who you are now does not match who you were, if you did not follow a direct path to something new. Your beliefs will need to grow with you.

DECEMBER 8
Seek what's sweet

It's important to cultivate the sweet and the soft
alongside our rougher and more resilient qualities.
Life requires a certain amount of toughness to
sustain our heart, which gets bumped and bruised as
we move through the world. Your tenderness is precious,
and your sweetness is worth preserving. Wear your
heart on your sleeve! Keeping yourself open despite the
hardness of the world is a form of strength.

DECEMBER 9
Count your blessings

Do you know how to count your blessings? Being aware
of what you have is empowering; knowing what you have
allows you to appreciate it with your full heart. You are
very blessed, a life full of inspiration and dreams, care and
excitement. Look for ways to share those blessings with
others, and build them into your routine. Make sharing
your blessings a part of counting them. After all, being
able to share is a blessing in and of itself.

DECEMBER 10
You are not alone

Reach out gently over the boundaries of your life into the lives of others. You are not alone, even in moments where you feel it must be so. The world is full of people who love you, even people who have not met you yet. And the people who do know you are waiting for you, even when each of us feels caught up in the web of our own lives. You do not have to wait for the people you love to come to you. It may not always be easy, but the connection with others will fill your heart. Even at a distance, your heart beats with others.

DECEMBER 11
Light your fire

An old tree falls in the forest, and it nourishes the ground around it, feeding the soil, providing shelter to what's small and crawling. Or a tree turns into a log, becomes firewood that fuels and feeds. It can crackle, sing, and dance in the flames, becoming something altogether new. What is no longer living can still give warmth, light, and joy to the living things around it. What in your life has faded that can be repurposed to bring new joy?

DECEMBER 12
Let the wind blow

The world turns and the wind blows, sometimes gently and sometimes harshly. The wind will howl, but you can withstand the gale. Build your foundations strong, reinforce the walls of your heart, the home where you live all the time. You do not need to let the drafts in; shut out the cold and keep yourself warm in the storm. Know that storms will pass, and no matter what wreckage they leave behind, your heart is sturdy enough to stand it. Everything can be rebuilt, even the house of your heart.

DECEMBER 13
Create warmth

The world gives you warmth in so many ways. Every piece of clothing that keeps you warm was woven and stitched thread by thread, yard by yard, into what you wrap around your body. How many hands held the clothing that holds you? Someone planted the seeds for the cotton, fed the lamb that grew your wool, cut and sewed every shirt in your closet. Even your warmest socks, likely knit by machine, had human hands touch it every step of the way.

DECEMBER 14
The world is still green

Some greens never fade, keeping hope alive even as the
world is cold. Tall evergreens and grasses, broad-leafed
bushes and narrow needles—these hard denizens of
the colder months are unstoppable. Even in their
dormancy, they remind us that green is the color of life,
of renewal, and a promise of warmer days. Look around
when you feel that the world is quiet and less alive in the
cold—you will be surprised by the number of plants that
still hold on to green, the pockets of grass and moss
that still hold on to the potential joys of spring yet
to come.

DECEMBER 15
Engage in conversation

Conversation is an exchange of energy and joy, ideas igniting ideas, inspiration lighting spirits across time and space. We have more options than ever to reach out and connect, crossing vast distances with electrons and excitement. The nature of our days is that they are filled with screens and news, moving quickly and asking so much of us. To speak with someone else about shared joys or concerns can slow it down, provide an anchor point for our spirit, and fill our cup with connection.

DECEMBER 16
Hug

Sometimes we cannot communicate our emotions in words, and only our bodies will do. When we embrace one another, we offer a kind of comfort and connection that comes from physicality. The warmth and solidity of our bodies together, the squeeze and pressure of one hand in another—our brains and bodies know the difference, and crave this special kind of connection. We often take the intimacy of touch for granted, but even the shake of a hand is a special moment of human interaction. In the right context, our bodies can provide joy, comfort, and expression that make up an entirely separate vocabulary we use to communicate.

DECEMBER 17
Look into the darkness

The days are shorter, cooler, and darker, but darkness can be a moment of rest. Without the light, we have time to reflect on days passed, and the light to come. Even the busiest person needs moments of quiet and rest, an opportunity to consider what they need and want, to process their experiences. The darkness is an opportunity, and it welcomes us, invites us to feel at home in a different way of being.

DECEMBER 18
The cold is temporary

Forming beauty drip by drip, icicles remind us that even the deepest winter is temporary and filled with beauty. The change and thaw can bring new joys in gradual waves and washes. Sun and ice may seem incompatible, but instead they can create something fantastical, beautiful, and prismatic out of the sharp snap of the cold. A fine edge, a sparkling decoration, icicles are a fleeting, temporary joy of the chill.

DECEMBER 19
Tomorrow will come

Whatever today brings, or has brought, tomorrow the sun rises on a new day. The tomorrows of your life stretch in front of you, waiting for you to try again. We all deserve to try again, and again. Perfection is a myth, but a new start is an opportunity to begin differently. You can take that opportunity every time it comes. Even if you need the next tomorrow, and the next, it will be there waiting for you.

DECEMBER 20
Touch is powerful

Human beings need one other. We are a deeply social species, and our bodies crave touch and connection. You can connect through touch with romantic partners, but touch is not exclusively romantic. Physical intimacy is part of every close human relationship—family, friends, even our pets. A desire to be close to one another, touching hands, exchanging hugs, a cool hand on a hot forehead—all forms of gentle and consensual touch are powerful conduits of the love we have for one another.

DECEMBER 21
The darkness can be joyful

Each year there is a day that is shortest, a solstice in which night dominates the hours and stretches out time. We celebrate the darkness of the night for the gifts of rest and reflection it brings. The light will return, but for now we appreciate the darkness for its own values. Once the longest night of the year passes, the days will grow longer with each night that follows, rolling slowing forward in the cycle toward spring. All you need to do to grow the days is wait patiently; they will grow on in their own time, like everything else in the spring.

DECEMBER 22
Cross the distance

The space between you and the people you love can cause an ache, but this is also a space to explore who you are on your own. There is no need to cultivate emotional distance across physical distance with the modern tools that surround us for communication. Reflect on what distances you create and what distances you can bridge by reaching out to others. Don't be afraid to look at the distance created as a productive boundary to explore your relationship to yourself, rather than one that locks you into loneliness.

DECEMBER 23
Feed others

Sharing food is a fundamental part of our celebrations and way of building community. From shared takeout to a communal meal in a restaurant to a home-cooked feast among friends, there are so many ways to share the food that brings us joy. When you have more than you need, invite others to the table. When your cupboards are full, can you share with others who may be in need? In this world, there is more than enough—how can you minimize what you waste and share what you have? Generosity with food builds strong communities and helps us take care of one another.

DECEMBER 24
Welcome celebration

Let yourself be light, let yourself be joyful. Does that sound radical to you? To seize joy where you find it is work in and of itself. Celebration is a precious commodity, and it is important to allow it into your life wherever you find it. It's not easy to be joyful in the world, but your joy is important. Safeguard your ability to celebrate, and spread it whenever you can. Bring others into your light, and lighten hearts wherever you go.

DECEMBER 25
Fire lights the darkness

Fire is changeable, transformative, and unpredictable.
It can burn or it can warm gently, it can rage with
consuming intensity or glow with a contained flame of a
candle. Watch it jump, dance, and catch others in its light
and heat. It has a strength and power that are totally
unique—the ability to reduce some materials to ash and
strengthen others. As with any power, it is how you wield
fire that shapes its transformations and impacts. You are
as powerful and changeable as any flame—make sure you
wield your own power with thoughtfulness and intention.

DECEMBER 26
Your sense of connection is its own support

Imagine each person who has touched your life stretching out across your days. Each of those people is tied to you in an invisible thread of fellowship and connection, shaping the path of your life. Each person has impacted you in ways big and small, spinning out into the space of the universe, supporting your existence. Can you feel them? They are still there, tied to you no matter where you go or how you change. Let them hold you and support you through whatever life brings.

DECEMBER 27
Take care of your body

You owe your body a debt of gratitude for all the ways in which it carries you through the world. It carries your heart, your mind, and your spirit. Are you caring for this vessel in all the ways that it needs? Caring for yourself is not all bubble baths and naps; sometimes it is the hard work of doing the laundry or feeding yourself a meal full of vegetables. It is not always as simple as drinking a glass of water, though it may be sometimes. Setting boundaries and setting goals is also self-care, the kind of care that allows you to show up for yourself and others. Ultimately, the care we take for ourselves can help us make the world a better place.

DECEMBER 28
Transform

Ashes aren't just ashes. What burns also rises, infused with lightness, rejoining the world. Energy and matter are not destroyed, not ever. The universe keeps building and transforming, every particle a puzzle piece, every fire a phoenix. When the world feels like it is burning around you, look for opportunities to transform and build. Use that energy to push you forward.

DECEMBER 29
An avalanche starts with one snowflake

A few snowflakes tremble and roll, collecting, shivering as they settle on the mountain. With a single shout, it can slide and race, razing the mountainside and destroying everything in its path. Who knew such small things could do so much? Every habit you shape is a snowflake that falls. Every action you take could shake the mountain. The avalanche can clear the way, creating change more powerful than you can imagine. Once it begins its slide, it cannot be stopped, so tread carefully with the changes you seek to trigger.

DECEMBER 30
Step into stillness

Take a breath right now. Can you feel it move through your body, filling your lungs and expanding your chest? As it leaves you, feel it move through, carrying out restlessness and anxiety. Rest here in this moment of stillness, without forcing forward motion. It's okay to be quiet for a moment and allow yourself the space to process. There is constant movement in our lives, a busyness that keeps us trapped in a dance of desires and needs, but any moment can become a still one if we invite that stillness in, even for just one breath.

DECEMBER 31
Surrender the past

The mind is a busy place filled with both our joys and our anxieties, constantly cycling through moments of the future we are afraid of and moments of the past we cannot release. It's absolutely okay to have these moments; it's part of being human. But the moments of worry cost us energy we could spend on other things that bring us joy, satisfaction, peace. It's also perfectly human to release them, giving them back to the universe. What worries can you relinquish for the moment?

In closing...

You've reached the end of this book, but not the end of your journey. Feel free to return to this book as often as you like, by following the dates one by one again or by dipping in and out as you like.

If you've found particular passages in this series of meditations valuable or meaningful to you, take the time to mark them so you can return to them easily. With entries for each day of the year, you can return to each in turn and still find new shades of meaning and resonance. If you do, you can start again with the first page, or follow along the calendar once again.

If you've kept a journal of your reflections on these daily entries, it can be a wonderful practice to return to these entries a year later when you've reached the same date. You can add new entries under the same date as last year, or continue with a new entry each day. Either way, it's a chance to guide your practice with the rhythm of the seasons and the natural cycles of the world around you.